Thomas Kerslake

Vestiges of the supremacy of Mercia in the South of England

During the eighth century

Thomas Kerslake

Vestiges of the supremacy of Mercia in the South of England
During the eighth century

ISBN/EAN: 9783742834041

Manufactured in Europe, USA, Canada, Australia, Japa

Cover: Foto ©Thomas Meinert / pixelio.de

Manufactured and distributed by brebook publishing software
(www.brebook.com)

Thomas Kerslake

Vestiges of the supremacy of Mercia in the South of England

VESTIGES OF

THE SUPREMACY OF MERCIA

IN THE SOUTH OF ENGLAND

DURING THE EIGHTH CENTURY

With T. Kerslake's Compliments,
Bristol, 1879.

CONTENTS.

ERRORS.

Pages 24, 25 in Notes; *for* p. 119—121, 125 *read* 15—17, 22.

,,   27. Note *for* 1565 *read* 1865.

,,   7, line 3, *for* "knut—" *read* "Knut—".

,,   11, 12, 34, *for* Bonifatius *prefer* Bonifacius.

,,   47, *for* appanage *read* apanage.

Various others, including some introduced after the proofs had been finally revised by the writer, by some one who fancied he knew the writer's meaning better than he knows it himself.

VESTIGES OF THE
SUPREMACY OF MERCIA
IN THE SOUTH OF ENGLAND
DURING THE EIGHTH CENTURY.

(Reprinted from the Transactions of the Bristol and Gloucester-shire Archæological Society).

Bristol, 1879.

VESTIGES OF THE SUPREMACY OF MERCIA IN THE SOUTH OF ENGLAND, DURING THE EIGHTH CENTURY.

By THOMAS KERSLAKE.

"............residual phenomena........., the small concentrated residues of great operations in the arts are almost sure to be the lurking-places of new chemical ingredients......It was a happy thought of Glauber to examine what everybody else threw away."—SIR J. F. W. HERSCHELL.

HAVING sometimes said that the date of the original foundation of the lately-demolished church of St. Werburgh, in the centre of the ancient walled town of Bristol, was the year 741, and that a building so called has, from that early date, always stood on that spot, I have been asked how I know it. I have answered; by the same evidence—and the best class of it—as the most important events of our national history, of the three centuries in which that date occurs, are known. That is, by necessary inference from the very scanty records of those times, confirmed by such topical monumental evidence as may have survived. But this fact in itself is, also, of considerable importance to our own local history; because, if it should be realized, it would be the very earliest solid date that has yet been attached to the place that we now call Bristol. We are accustomed to speak, with a certain amount of popular pride, of "Old Bristol," and in like manner of "Old England," but without considering which is the oldest of the two. The position here attempted would give that precedence to Bristol.

It need scarcely be mentioned that what we now call England is no other than an enlargement of the ancient kingdom of the West Saxons, by the subjugation and annexation of the other kingdoms of the southern part of the island. A subjugation of which the result is that our now ruling sovereign is the successor, as well as descendant, of the Saxon Kings of Wessex, and of the supremacy which they ultimately achieved. Of course this was only the final effect of a long series of political revolutions. It was preceded by others that had promised a different upshot : one of which was the long-threatened supremacy of the Anglian kingdom of Mercia ; by Penda, a Pagan king, and afterwards, during the long reigns of Æthelbald and Offa, his christian successors in his kingdom and aggressive policy.

One of two fates awaits a supplanted dynasty : to be traduced, or to be forgotten. Although this milder one has been the lot of the Mercian Empire, yet it is believed that distinct, and even extensive, traces can still be discerned, beyond the original seat of its own kingdom, of its former supremacy over the other kingdoms of England. In fact, this name itself of " England," still co-extensive with this former Anglian supremacy over the Saxons, is a glorious monumental legacy of that supremacy, which their later Saxon over-rulers never renounced, and which has become their password to the uttermost parts of the earth.

But it is with the encroachments of Æthelbald upon Wessex that we are in the first instance concerned. South of Mercia proper was another nation called Huiccia, extending over the present counties of Worcester and Gloucester, with part of Warwickshire and Herefordshire, and having the Bristol river Avon for its southern boundary. It is barely possible that it may have included a narrow margin between that river and the Wans-dyke, which runs along the south of that river, at a parallel of from two to three miles from it ; but of this no distinct evidence has been found. Some land, between the river and Wansdyke, did in fact belong to the Abbey of Bath, which is itself on the north of the river, but that this is said to have been bought—" mercati sumus digno practio "—from Kenulf, King of the West Saxons[1], makes it likely that it was the river that had been the tribal boundary.

Until divided from Gloucester by King Henry VIII., the

[1] Cod. Dip. CXLIII.

B 2

Bishopric of Worcester substantially continued the territory, and the present name of Worcester = Wigorceaster = Wigorniæ civitas (A.D. 789), no doubt transmits, although obscurely, the name of Huiccia ; and the church there contained (A.D. 774) " pontificalis Cathedra Huicciorum." The name may even remain in " Warwick," and especially in " Wickwar " = Huiccanwaru ; but such instances must not be two much trusted, as there are other fruitful sources of " wick," in names. In Worcestershire names, however, "-wick " and "-wich " as testimonials are abundant. Droitwich = " Uuiccium emptorium " (A.D. 715), almost certainly is so derived, in spite of its ambiguous contact with the great etymological puzzle of the "Saltwiches." [1]

At all events, within a hundred years from Ceawlin's first subjugation of it, Saxon Wiccia had become entirely subject to Anglian Mercia. But there can be no doubt that its earliest Teutonic settlers were West Saxons. Even now, any one of us West Saxons, who should wander through Gloucestershire and Worcestershire, would recognise his own dialect. He would, perhaps, say they " speak finer" up here, but he would feel that his ears are still at home. If he should, however, advance into Derbyshire, or Staffordshire, or Eastern Shropshire, he would encounter a musical cadence, or song, which, though far from being unpleasant from an agreeable voice, would be very strange to him. He would, in fact, have passed out of Wiccia into Mercia proper : from a West-Saxon population into one of original Anglian substratum.

What was the earlier political condition of Wiccia before it fell under the dominion of Mercia : whether it was ever for any time an integral part of the kingdom of Wessex, or a distinct

[1] Dr. Lappenburg (I. 38) describes the people of Warwickshire and Worcestershire as the "Gewissi." But the "Gevissæ" was the ancient name of the southern main stem of the West Saxons, who made their way into Somerset and Devon (Bæda. H. E. III. 7), and plainly a name of distinction from the Huiccii. All the pre-Christian pedigrees of the West Saxon leaders have an early name "Gewis," which has been, with great likelihood, supposed to have been the origin of the name of the Gevissæ. In some only of the pedigrees, this name is next preceded by "Wig." This seems to point to a division of the leadership between two kinsmen, perhaps brothers ; and the Wiccii or Wigornians to be derived from the latter.

subregulate of it, is uncertain. Two of the earlier pagan West-Saxon inroads (A.D. 577-584) were of this region, and happened long before that race had penetrated Somerset. It is not to be believed that any part of later Somerset, south of Avon, was included in either of these two pagan conquests of Ceawlin ; nor even the south-west angle of Gloucestershire itself, that forms the separate elevated limestone ridges between the Bristol Frome and the Severn. There are some other reasons for believing that these heights immediately west of Bristol—say, Clifton, Henbury, and northward along the Ridgeway to about Tortworth—remained, both Welsh and Christian, for nearly a century afterwards ; and that they were only reduced to Teutonic rule along with the subjection of Saxon Wiccia itself to Anglian Mercia. The record in the Anglo-Saxon Chronicle of the conquest of A.D. 577 plainly indicates the course of it, by the names of the places concerned—Bath, Dyrham, Cirencester, and Gloucester. It was not any river that was the instrument of advance ; but, flanked and supported by the ancient Foss-way, the continuous elevated table-land of the southern limb of the Cotswolds, still abounding with remains of military occupations of yet earlier peoples. This is separated from the more western height by a broad belt of low land, then a weald or forest, since known as Kingswood ; which, the line of the places named in the annal of the conquest, plainly indicates to have been purposely avoided : the district west of it, therefore still continued British. As to Ceawlin's second expedition, A.D. 584, it most probably extended from Gloucester to the country between Severn and Wye, as far as Hereford,[1] and into the now Saxon-speaking Worcestershire. But that Ceawlin followed the Severn, and penetrated Cheshire to an unimportant place called "Faddiley," is not only unlikely, but rests entirely on a single philological argument, concerning that name, too refined and unpractical for the burden laid upon it[2], and inconsistent with the later associations of the name itself.

But if Wiccia became West-Saxon in 577-584, it did not long remain undisturbed by its Anglian northern neighbour. About

[1] A.S. Chron., "Feathan leag"—Welsh Chronicles, "*Ffery llwy.*"

[2] Dr. Guest in Archæological Journal, vol. XIX., p. 197.

fifty years later (A.D. 628), it is recorded in the Chronicle, that the rulers of Wessex and Mercia, fought at Cirencester, "and then compromised." This shews that hitherto, for fifty years, all Wiccia had been ruled by Wessex : also that, except what reduction of territory may be represented by a Mercian inroad as far as Cirencester, it still continued under Wessex. But although this exception itself did not last many years longer, this is enough to account for our finding a Saxon people under Anglian government. In another fifty years, Wiccia is found to have become a sub-regulate, governed by Mercian sub-kings, and constituted a separate Bishopric, an offshoot from Mercian Lichfield ; and from that time the kings of Mercia and their sub-reguli are found dealing with lands in various parts of Wiccia, even to the southern frontier, as at Malmesbury and Bath ; and by a charter of Æthelred, King of Mercia, dated by Dr. Hickes, A.D. 692, the newly instituted cathedral in the city of Weogorna, is endowed with land at a place well-known to us by what was, even then said to be an "ancient name," Henbury ("vetusto vocabulo nuncupatur heanburg."[1])

Much needless demur, if not excitement, has of late years been stirred up by some of the learned,[2] at the name "Anglo-Saxon," for the oldest condition of English. They allege that this designation is "a most unlucky one," and that in the first half of this century it was the cause of a "crass ignorance" of the true relations of continuity in this nation before and after the Norman conquest. Those who remember that time, well know that this imputed ignorance did not prevail : that if the most ordinary schoolboy, had then been asked, why William was called "the Conqueror," he would have at once, rightly or wrongly, answered "because he conquered us," and that he was only less detested than "Buonaparte," because he was at that time farther away. They have now lived to be astonished to find that, by their own confession, the higher scholars of this later age are terrified by a fear of confusion

[1] Thesaurus, I. 169.

[2] Dr. Guest and Mr. Freeman, and their followers, as the Saturday Review, and the various school histories, which, having adopted the innovation, are lauded in that journal.

in this rudimentary piece of learning. So these learned men put themselves into the most ludicrous passions, and—let us try to humour them—King " knut "-like scoldings at the tide, and Dame Partingtonian mop-twirlings, to cure us of such a dangerous old heresy. For old it is, and deeply rooted. Those " Anglo-Saxon " kings who assumed the supreme rule of the kingdoms of both races, so called themselves : and the entire "Anglo-Saxon" literature has been only so known in modern Europe, for the last three centuries ; not only at home, but in Germany, Denmark, France, and where-ever it has ever appeared in print. Yet another most learned and acute and sober Professor has been lately tempted to join the "unlucky" cry : saying that " It is like calling Greek, Attico-Ionian."[1] Why " Greek ? " Why not " Hellenic ? " Is not " Greek " an exotic, and as barbarous as " Attico-Ionian " or " Anglo-Saxon ? "

But in our concern with the Wiccians we are exempt from this newly raised dispute. Here we have a great colony of a Saxon people who very soon fell under the dominion of Anglian kings, and so remained until a later revolution, the final supremacy of Wessex, made them once more Saxon subjects. The Wiccians, at any rate however, had become literally Anglo-Saxon : a Saxon people under Anglian rule. Shakespear was a Wiccian, born and bred—if one, who has taught us so much more than any breeding could have taught him, can be said to have been bred amongst us—at any rate he was born a Wiccian, and thereby an Anglo-Saxon, in the natural and indisputable sense : a sense earlier, stricter, and more real than that which afterwards extended the phrase to the entire kingdom. Wiccia was no doubt colonized by the Saxons, while the Saxons were yet pagan ; and afterwards christianized by their Anglian Mercian subjugators. Not so the Saxons of Somerset, who were already christians when they first penetrated that province.[2]

Subsequent annals of the Chronicle shew that Wessex long remained impatient of the loss of Wiccia. In A.D. 715, a battle is shortly mentioned at a place, usually, and not impossibly, said

[1] Prof. W. W. Skeat, Macmillan, Feb. 1879, p. 313.
[2] See " A Primæval British Metropolis," Bristol, 1877, pp. 45-80.

to be Wanborough, a remarkable elevation within the fork of two great Roman ways a few miles south of Swindon. But our business is with three later entries in the Chronicle, for the three successive years 741, 742, and 743; of which the first for A.D. 741, will be first here submitted as the record of the final sub-jection of Wiccia, and the establishment of the Bristol Avon as the permanent southern frontier of Mercia. The other two Annals will then be otherwise disposed of.

These are the words of the Chronicle :—

A.D. 741. Now Cuthred succeeded to the West-Saxon king-dom, and held it sixteen years, and he contended hardly with Æthelbald, King of the Mercians.

A.D. 742. Now was a great Synod gathered at Cloveshou, and Æthelbald, King of the Mercians was there, and Cutbert, Archbishop [of Canterbury], and many other wise men.

A.D. 743. Now Æthelbald, King of the Mercians, and Cuthred, King of the West-Saxons fought with the Welsh.

We have in these three Annals a specimen of that condensed form and style, that is common to this ancient text and still more venerable primæval records; and which invites and justifies attempts to interpret them by the help of any existing external monuments.

There are still known in England thirteen dedications of churches or chapels in the name of St. Werburgh, although, perhaps, not more than half of them are any longer above ground.[1] Seven, however, out of the thirteen are within the counties of Stafford, Chester, Shropshire, and Derbyshire : that is, they are within the original kingdom of Mercia, wherein, as the posthumous renown of the saint never extended beyond a nation, or rather a dynasty, that long since has been extinct and forgotten, we might

---

[1] One of the obsolete ones was brought to mind by a paper read by Mr. C. E. Davis, at Bath, in 1857 : another is printed from the Register of Worcester Cathedral in Thomas's Survey, kindly pointed out by Mr. John Taylor ; so that others, unreckoned, may possibly be brought to light.

There is one, in addition to all those above mentioned, at Dublin ; but, as the dedications in Strongbow's Dublin are no more than a post-Norman colonisation of those at Bristol, it does not enter into our reckoning.

have expected to have found them all. But the other six are extraneous, and three of them great stragglers. These must have owed their origin to political and military extensions of the influence of that kingdom, and these, it is intended to show, are found in places where Æthelbald, one of the three Mercian aspirants for English empire, has made good a conquest. This dedication may, therefore, be believed to have been his usual method of making his mark of possession.

St. Werburgh was the daughter of Wulfhere, the second christian King of Mercia, who was the son of Penda, the last pagan King. Æthelbald was the grandson of Eawa, a brother of Penda, probably the Eoba, who, in the Annales Cambriæ, A.D. 644, is himself called "rex Merciorum;" so that Æthelbald and Werburgh were what we should call second cousins.[1] Wulfhere, A.D. 675, was succeeded by his brother Æthelred, who placed his niece Werburgh at the head of three great convents of women, with a sort of general spiritual charge of the female portion of the newly christianised kingdom. She is said to have died about A.D. 700, for it is noted that on opening her coffin in the year 708, her body, after eight years, was found unaltered, and her vestments undefiled; and from this time, sealed by this reputed miracle, the renown of her sanctity soon grew to beatification; and when, eight

[1] The genealogical relation of St. Werburgh and Æthelbald will be seen in this extract from Dr. Lappenberg's Pedigree of the Kings of Mercia·

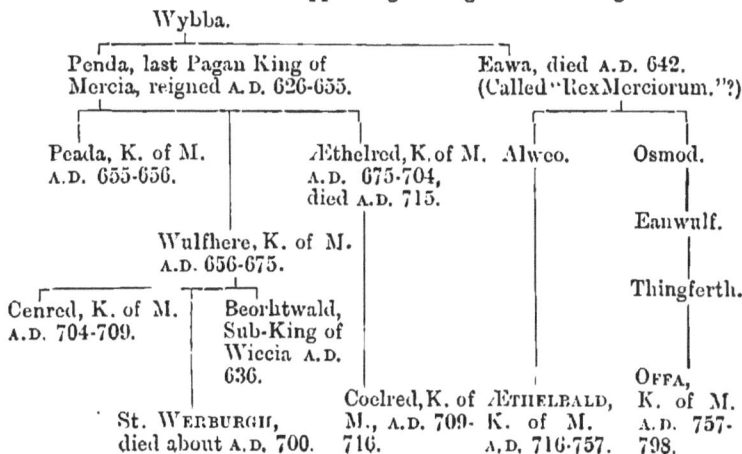

Wybba.

Penda, last Pagan King of Mercia, reigned A.D. 626-655. Eawa, died A.D. 642. (Called "Rex Merciorum."?)

Peada, K. of M. A.D. 655-656. Æthelred, K. of M. A.D. 675-704, died A.D. 715. Alweo. Osmod.

Wulfhere, K. of M. A.D. 656-675. Eanwulf.

Cenred, K. of M. A.D. 704-709. Beorhtwald, Sub-King of Wiccia A.D. 636. Thingferth.

St. Werburgh, died about A.D. 700. Coelred, K. of M., A.D. 709-716. Æthelbald, K. of M. A.D. 716-757. Offa, K. of M. A.D. 757-798.

years afterwards, her kinsman Æthelbald began his reign, she had
achieved the reputation and precedence of the latest national
saint. She was, however, one of a family of whom many of the
women have transmitted their names, from immediately after their
deaths to our own times, attached to religious foundations. Among
these, that of her aunt, St. Audry, still lives in Ely Cathedral :
and this example may serve as a crutch to those who find it hard
to realise the unbroken duration of churches, with these names,
direct from the very ages in which the persons who bore them
lived ; for the continuity of this name at Ely is a matter of open
and undisputed history, unaided by mere inference, such as our less
conspicuous case requires. There are some, also, who stumble at
finding all the female saints of particular provinces to have been
members of one royal family. But of this we have an analogy
pervading the entire area of our own every-day life, in the active
assistance in all benevolent purposes, received by the clergyman of
nearly every parish, from the leisured daughters of the more
wealthy families. In those missionary days, the kingdoms of the
newly-converted rulers were the only parishes, and the king and
his family were as the squire and his family are now ; and the
greater lustre, which then shone out around the name of each, was
as that of a little candle, in their wider world, compared with what
would be its effect in a general illumination now. The earlier
British churches have presented us with the same phenomenon.
The numerous progeny, of children and grand-children, of Brychan
of Brecknock, have nearly all left their names in many churches
in South Wales, and even in the opposite promontory of Cornwall
and Devon.

The historical facts of the name and local fame of this royal
personage are all that we are concerned with. Otherwise, in some
later times, it has been adorned with the usual amount of miraculous fable. The most notable of the miracles credited to her is,
that one of her corn-fields being continually ravaged by flocks of
geese, at her mere command they went into voluntary exile. As
this is said to have happened near Chester, it is easy to refer the
story to the monks there, who alone were interested in gilding her

shrine with it ; and her relics were not translated there till nearly
two hundred years after her death. At any rate, the citizens of
Bristol are living witnesses that her name is no safeguard of her
heritage against the devastations of wasteful bipeds, who are not
only unwise, but also unfledged. This imputed miracle is more
transparent than is always the case with such embellishments of
the lives of those who were the first to accept the new faith, and
to promote it with active earnestness. In it may, at once, be discerned an ordinary incident of her pastoral or predial economy,
exaggerated to a miracle in an age which preferred supernatural
to natural causes.

The career of Æthelbald is, of course, more widely known,
holding, as it does, a prominent place in the general history of the
times. His reign extended from A.D. 716 to 755, and was chiefly
employed in extending his sovereignty by the subjugation of neighbouring kingdoms, and by his munificent patronage of the church.
In the first year of his reign, he at once showed a disposition to
commemorate his own friends, by dedicating churches in their
names, by using this method of perpetuating, at Croyland, the
recent memory of Guthlac, his kinsman and protector in exile.
It seems, however, that the pagan manners of the northern myth-
ology are not purged for several generations after conversion : but,
as appears from another example, of the practical paganism of the
Dukes of Normandy, down to our William the Mamzer, unless
attended with more than the average cruelty and injustice of the
times, meet with only a qualified reproach, until they are in
conflict with church discipline and law. The celebrated severe,
but friendly and respectful epistolary rebuke from Bonifatius,[1]

---

[1] The birth, in the West of England, of this assiduous propagator of
the great mediæval embodiment of civilisation, zealous devotee of the
Church, and prominent European statesman, is so important a fact in our
ethnical topography as to deserve a passing, though attentive, glance.
On the authority of those who personally knew him, he was born near
Exeter, about the year 680 ; but, although no Saxon Conquest had yet
extended so far westward, he bore a Saxon name, although in the midst of
a Celtic people. From this, and from other circumstances also mentioned
of his early life, it may be inferred that his father was a peaceful Saxon
colonist, in advance of conquest, and still a pagan; and that his mother was
a British Christian. He is, therefore, the earliest recorded example of that

Archbishop of Mainz, contains a heavy indictment against both
Æthelbald and his predecessor Coelred, and their courts, while
irrepressible compound of the two races that has since made so many deep
and broad marks upon the outer world. This fact, of a pacific international
intercourse antecedent to conquest, was so directly in conflict with evolved
history, that it has provoked an ineffectual attempt to subvert the testimony of it, by questioning the undoubted reading of the name as being
that of Exeter. (E. A. Freeman, Esq., in Archæol. Journal, vol. xxx., or
Macmillan M., Sep. 1873, p. 474).

Another, but later, testimony gives us the name of the place near
Exeter where he was born : Crediton, in a deep and most fertile valley of
that middle district in Devon which is the interval between the highlands
of Dartmoor and Exmoor, but rather to the south-west of that district.
Here there is reason to believe Christianity had already been established at a much earlier time, by Croyde, or Creed, an Irish missionary
virgin, who has left her name at other places throughout both Devon and
Cornwall. The incredulity, that Crediton was the birthplace of S. Bonifatius, was vindicated by saying that it has "no *ancient* authority whatever."
It has not contemporary authority like that for "near Exeter," which,
however, it strongly confirms, and which, for English topography of so
early a date, is almost unique in its explicitness, but it has an authority as
ancient as we are obliged to be content with for nearly all we know of those
times, and far more respectable than most of it. The authority is a church-
service book, still preserved in Exeter Cathedral, compiled by Bp. Gran-
disson (died A.D. 1366), and attested by his autograph. If this had been a
mere outdoor tradition, and had rested upon no more than the personal
authority of this most distinguished man, it would even then have been the
very highest evidence of its kind. But it does no such thing. Bp. Gran-
disson is not the *author* of the book any more than St. Osmund is the
author of the Usages of Sarum. He is the codifier of the immemorial obser-
vances of the church, at which the contemporary biographer of St. Boniface attests that he received his earliest teaching ; and of the very existence
of which church their irreproachable attestation is by a long interval the
earliest record.

But there is another evidence that this great man of his age was
known, to his compatriots in his own province, as one of themselves. Of
this they have left a substantial monument in the dedications of two
churches still remaining in Devon, not in his ecclesiastical name, by which
the rest of the world knew him, but in his birth-name of "Winfrid" by
which they had remembered him. The two more distant extant dedications
of Bonchurch, Isle of Wight, and Banbury, Cheshire, on the contrary, in
their dedications of "St. Boniface" are mere reflections of his realised
continental greatness back upon his own island.

Winfrith, near Lulworth, in Dorset, probably had a third western example
of the dedication, for although the present church is of Norman structure,
and with a different dedication (St. Christopher), most likely, as in many
other cases, an earlier sanctuary existed in Winfrid's name.

it acknowledges his prosperity, munificence to the church, and his just administration.

Having these specially national or tribal circumstances in view, it is thought that the six dedications of St. Werburgh that are found beyond the original Mercia must have had special causes, which it is believed can be found in the transactions that are recorded in the three successive Annals of the Chronicle above recited ; and that the dedications and the Annals will therefore be found to mutually account for each other. The seven churches within Mercia, without any doubt each has its own history, mostly connected with Æthelbald : perhaps all except the present Chester Cathedral, which arose out of the translation, nearly two hundred years later, of her relics to that place, from her original shrine in one of her three convents. But these home dedications do not fall within our purview, which is limited to the wanderers.

When the Chronicle, A.D. 741, says that Cuthred of Wessex contended with Æthelbald of Mercia, it can only mean that he attempted a reprisal of some portion of Wiccia : but it appears from the Annal of 743, that in the two years the combatants had become allies. The frontier between Mercia and Wessex had been finally determined ; and there we find the name of Æthelbald's recently beatified kinswoman, thrice repeated, along his own north bank of the Avon—at Bath, at Bristol, and at Henbury. It should be noticed that otherwise than these three, thus placed with an obvious purpose, none whatever are found throughout the whole length and breadth of Wiccia, the other seven being scattered within Mercia proper.[1] It is hence inferred that these three dedications are contemporary with each other, and the immediate result of the transaction of A.D. 741. It may also be worth noting that one of the still surviving dedications of St. Werburgh within Mercia, at

---

[1] What may be presumed to be another dedication of St. Werburgh has since been traced to its place, and may be reckoned as an eighth of those in the home kingdom, at its southern frontier. Among the land-marks (A.D. 849) of a place called "Coftun," is Werburgh's cross ("in Wærburge rode") Cod. Dip. CCLXII. This has been found to be Coftou Hackett, in that north point of Worcestershire that abuts upon Stafford-shire and Shropshire.

Warburton, is similarly situated within the northern frontier, the river Mersey; and probably records a similar result of Æthelbald's inroad of Northumbria, entered in the Chronicle at the earlier date of 737 : also, according to Bæda, A.D. 740.[1]

The St. Werburgh at Bath is no longer in existence, but its site is still on record. It was less than a quarter of a mile north of the Roman town, and about a quarter of a mile from the departure of the western Roman road, now called Via Julia, from the Foss Way, and between them, and very near to both.[2]

What was the condition of the spot now occupied by Bristol, in the centre of which, until yesterday, for nearly eleven hundred and fifty years, the church with this name has stood, when it was first planted there, this is not the place to discuss. A century-and-a-half earlier (A.D. 577), Bath, as we have seen, had been occupied by the West Saxons, and had no doubt so continued, until this advance southward of Æthelbald's frontier also absorbed that city, or certainly its northern suburb, into Mercia. A great highway, of much earlier date than the times here being considered, skirted the southern edge of the weald that we only know as Kingswood; and at least approached the neck of the peninsula—projecting into a land-locked tidal lagoon, not a swamp, flooded by the confluence, at the crest of the tide, of Frome and Avon—upon which stands Bristol, and which has been hitherto crowned with Æthelbald's usual symbol of Mercian dominion. As long ago as ships frequented the estuary of the Severn—ages before the times we are considering—it is inconceivable that the uncommon advantages of this haven could have been unknown. A British city had, no doubt, already existed for unknown ages on the neighbouring heights west of the lagoon; and there is a reason, too long to set forth here, to believe that the sheltered Bristol peninsula itself was used, by the West-Saxons of Ceawlin's settlement at Bath, as an advanced frontier towards the Welsh of West Gloucestershire, long before it was appropriated by Mercia. It was, perhaps, already a town before Æthelbald planted upon it one of his limitary sanctuaries, having, *more Saxonico*, a fortress on the isthmus, upon which

---

[1] Lib. v.   [2] See Warner p. 228. Collinson's Som., vol. I. Bath, p. 53.

the great square Norman tower of Robert the Consul was afterwards raised.

All that is known of the sanctuary at Henbury is, that it was one of the chapels to Westbury, confirmed to Worcester Cathedral by Bp. Simon (A.D. 1125-50), and is described in his charter as " capella sancte Wereburge super montem Hembiric sita."[1] This is in that south-western limb of Gloucestershire, bounded by the Frome, Avon, and Severn, and separated by Kingswood Forest, which it has already been suggested was never Saxon, but remained Welsh until subdued by Mercia.

So that as the only examples of this dedication to be found south of Staffordshire and Derbyshire, are the three which line the north shore of the Avon, the new frontier of Wessex and Mercia; the entire district of Gloucestershire, Worcestershire, and all the intervening country, from east to west, being totally without them ; these three are manifestly arrayed in one line for a special purpose. The record, of the contest of Wessex and Mercia, contained in the Annal of A.D. 741, is thus accounted for in this monument of its result. Three more distant St. Werburghs remain, of which two will now be appropriated to that of A.D. 743. The one for A.D. 742, passed over for the present, will afterwards be shewn to involve the remaining sixth.

It will be remembered that, in the year 743, the Chronicle shews Æthelbald and Cuthred, who two years earlier had been fighting each other, now united, by perhaps an analogue of a Russo-Turkish alliance, against an enemy who, while Cuthred had been engaged with his Teutonic rival, had become troublesome in his rear, and dangerous to both. Under this year, 743, it says " Now Æthelbald King of the Mercians and Cuthred King of the West Saxons fought with the Welsh." It does not say which of the then surviving three great bodies of the Welsh, who had been pressed into the great western limbs of the island, that are geographically divided from each other by the estuary of the Severn and

---

[1] Thomas, Worc. Cath., 1736, Append. No. 9. p. 6. It might be worth while to search for remains of it in plantations thereabout. It is distinct from the chapel of St. Blaise, and on a different eminence.

the great bay of Lancashire; but none can be meant but the
Damnonian or Cornish Britons—the "Welsh" of the West Saxon
Cuthred. No more of Devon could then have been held by the
West Saxons than the fruitful southern lowlands, easily accessible
from Somerset and Dorset, and from the south-coast. Most or all
of Cornwall, and the highlands of Dartmoor and Exmoor, extend
ing into north-west Somerset, still remained British or Welsh; as
for the most part in blood, though not in speech, they do to
this day.

Written history is silent as to the parts separately taken by
the allies in this contest; but other tokens of that of the Mercian
are extant; and the two dedications of St. Werburgh that will next
engage us are among the most significant. A glance at Mercia
and the extent of the provinces annexed thereto by conquest,
betrays a ruling political aim at obtaining access to the great
seaports. Besides the Humber with Trent, and the Mersey, and,
as we shall see below, the Medway, and the Thames itself; what
is more to our purpose, we have found it already in possession of
Bristol, added to Gloucester and the mouth of the Wye. An
aggressive kingdom, with this policy, needs no chronicle to
tell us that ships were abundant; and that at least it must
have been able to command the transport service of a large
mercantile fleet. It will readily be understood that one of
Æthelbald's strategics, in aid of his ally against his Damnonian
insurgents, would be, to outflank the ally himself; and establish
a cordon across his rear. This was effected by transporting, from
his Wiccian ports on the Severn, to the north coast of Devon, a
large migration of his own people; who not only occupied the district between the Dartmoor highlands and the north coast, not
yet Teutonized by Wessex; but possessed themselves of the entire
line across the western promontory, between Dartmoor and the
Tamar, as far as the south sea near Plymouth.

Of this strategic movement several strong indications remain
upon the face of the district; which it is thought, mutually derive
increased force from their accumulation. One of them is the
existence, at the outposts of this expedition, of two of Æthelbald's
favourite dedications of his kinswoman. One, at Warbstow, stands

at the western extremity of an incroachment of about eight miles
beyond the Tamar, near Launceston, into Cornwall—still visible
in our county maps, in the abstraction of an entire parish from
the western side of the otherwise frontier river, by an abnormal
projection beyond it. The other is at Wembury, where the church
is finely situated on the sea-cliff of the eastern lip of Plymouth
Sound. These two examples of the dedication, which was the
favourite stamp of the conqueror's heel, mark therefore the
western and southern extremities of the assumed invasion.

Another trace of this great unwritten Mercian descent upon
Damnonia, may be discerned in the structure, as well as the constituents, of the place-names that cover the invaded district. The
country, between the central highlands of Devon and the north-west
coast of Devon and north-east of Cornwall, is not only secluded into
an angular area bounded by the sea ; but lies quite out of the course
of the torrent of West Saxon advance westward : which indeed
had been evidently checked by the Dartmoor heights. It might
have been expected, therefore, except for the explanation now
offered, that this district would have retained a strong tincture of
its original Celtic condition, in that lasting index of race-occupancy
its place-names. In this respect it might have presented the
appearance of having been conquered, but not of a complete re-
placement of population. On the contrary, at the first glance of a
full-named map, or in a passage through it, the entire district is
surprisingly English. Besides this, the place-names have not only
conspicuous peculiarities of structure, that at once distinguish this
district from that of the West Saxons south and east of Dartmoor ;
but these recur with such uncommon frequency and uniformity,
stopped by almost arbitrary limits, as to be manifestly due to a
simultaneous descent of a very large population, at once spreading
themselves over the whole of an extensive region.

One of these notes of a great and simultaneous in-migration, is the
termination of names in " -worthy ;" which literally swarms over
the entire tract of country between the Torridge and the Tamar
It is continued with no less frequency into that abnormal loop of
the Devon frontier, which having crossed the Tamar stretches away

c

towards the St. Werburgh dedication at Warbstow, and may be
assumed to have been afterwards conceded to a condensed English
speaking population already in possession; when, two hundred
years later, King Athelstan determined that frontier. Others of
these names are found scattered down southwards, over the
western foot of Dartmoor, towards the southern St. Werburgh at
Wembury, near Plymouth Sound. It is thought that this Devonshire "-worthy" is a transplant of the "-wardine" or "-uerdin"
so frequent on the higher Severn and the Wye; changed during
the long weaning from its cradle. In Domesday Book the
orthography of the Devonshire "-worthys" and the "-wardines"
of Worcestershire, Herefordshire, and Shropshire, was still almost
identical, and their orthographical variations flit round one centre
common to both. There is a "Heneverdon" at Plympton, close
to Wembury.

Another ending of names, also noticeable on the score of
constant repetition over this large though limited area, is "-stow,"
found annexed to the names of church-towns as the equivalent of
the Cornish prefix "Lan-" and the Welsh "Llan-." Another very
numerous termination is "-cot." But, with regard to these two,
it should be mentioned, as a remarkable difference from the case
of "-worthy," that "-worthy" almost ceases abruptly with the
Tamar boundary, except that it follows the Devon encroachments
above mentioned across that river; whilst the "-stow" and
"-cot" continue over the north-east angle of Cornwall itself to the
sea. Although this observation does not conflict with our Mercian
in-migration, it is not accounted for by it. It may indicate
successive expeditions or reinforcements, after Æthelbald's; occurr-
ing as they do beyond his Warbstow outpost. One incident of this
disregard of the frontier, occurs in a difference of the behaviour of
"-stow" on the two sides of it, and may be worth noting for its
own sake. On the Devon side of the Tamar is a "Virginstow,"
with a dedication of St. Bridget: on the Cornish side of the
boundary is "Morwenstow," preserving "morwen," understood
to be the Cornish word for "virgin." So that this English "-stow"
is found added to both the English and the Cornish name, each

derived from a pre-existent church, dedicated to a female saint.
The dedication of the present Morwenstow church appears to be
uncertain; but Dr. Borlase and Dr. Oliver have both found, in
Bishop Stafford's Register, note of a former chapel of St. Mary
in the parish.

It is not meant that these three name-marks are not to be
found in other parts of England : on the contrary, we shall here-
after see Mercian operations in other counties sufficient to account
for a very wide sprinkling of them. What is here dwelt upon is the
unexampled crowding of them, showing simultaneous colonisation
upon a great scale. Another, but smaller, group of " -worthy "
and " -cot," occurs on the Severn coast of Somerset, about Minehead, indicating another naval descent of Mercia. In fact, although
the great swarm above described occurs between 'the Torridge and
the Tamar, two distinct trains flow from it : one, as before said,
over the west foot of Dartmoor to the south sea : another along the
Severn coast, eastward, ending with the Minehead or Selworthy
group; and does not crop up again until in Gloucestershire it is
found in its home midland form of Sheepwardine, and Miserden.

Another example of this sort of connection of Mercia with
Cornwall and south-west England may be briefly cited. Among
the few — not more than six or eight—non-Celtic, but national or
non-Catholic, dedications in Cornwall, is one of St. Cuthbert ; a
name that is also continued in " Cubert," the secular name of the
town. It is situated in one of the promontories that so boldly pro-
ject into the sea on the north coast of Cornwall, but farther westward than the English footsteps above noted. A very learned and
acute writer[1] could not make out how " St. Cuthbert has made his
way from Lindisfarn to Wells ; " and says, perhaps truly, that it
" does not imply a Northumbrian settlement in Somerset." But St.
Cuthbert at Wells, might reasonably be left to the cross-examina-
tion of historians, or neighbours, of that place ; and if judiciously
and reverently questioned, by the help of what is here said, would
possibly give a good account of himself.

It is quite true, as might have been expected, that St. Cuthbert

[1] Saturday Rev., Ap. 24, 1875, p. 533.

c 2

is much more often found at his home in Northumbria than
in the south-west of England. In the south-eastern counties he
has not been found at all : but over the midland counties, and all
down through the western ones he is thinly sprinkled all the way.
Between Humber and Mersey, and Tweed and Solway, forty-three
can be named if required, and Bishop Forbes adds many from his side
of the border. Derbyshire has one at Doveridge, near the Mercian
royal castle of Tutbury ; Warwickshire one at Shustoke, eight
miles south of another villa regia at Tamworth ; Leicestershire,
Notts, Beds, have each one ; Lincoln and Norfolk two each ;
Worcestershire perhaps one in the name " Cudbergelawe ; "[1] Gloucestershire, one at Siston by Pucklechurch, and probably a second
in the name " Cuberley ; " Herefordshire two, or three ? Somerset
one at Wells ; Dorset one, or two ? Devon one, Cornwall one.

This condensed statement of a series of facts, constitutes one of
the phenomena of our argument ; and shall here be accounted for
by an observation, to which there will, further on, be occasion to
revert. Whatever may have been the causes, there was a more
intimate earlier intercourse between the Anglian kingdoms of
Northumbria and Mercia, than between them and the more southern
or Saxon kingdoms ; so that, in fact, the hagiology of Northumberland is found to have infiltrated into that of Mercia. Sometimes
the intercourse was hostile, and of this St. Oswald's prevalence in
Cheshire, Shropshire, &c., is an instance historically known.
Another cause might be collected from a study of any pedigree
tables of the rulers of the two kingdoms. A later action of this
mutuality appears in the dedications of the Northumbrian Alk-
mond, found in towns built by Æthelfled, who, Amazon though
she be reputed, confessed her womanhood in her *cultus* of the
child-martyr, as at her town of Derby and Shrewsbury. When,
therefore, we find Northumbrian dedications in these unlikely
southern regions, we are not driven to "imply a Northumbrian
settlement," but a sprout of Northumbrian hagiology, replanted
along with a Mercian settlement.

Midway between Wells and Somerton is Glastonbury. The

---

[1] Reg. Worc. Priory, Camden Soc.

Chronicle published by Hearne as John of Glastonbury, says that
Æthelbald "rex Merciorum," A.D. 744, gave to Abbot Tumbert,
and the Familia at Glaston, lands at "Gassing and Bradelegh "[1]
Bradley is known and plain enough, and adjoins the Foss Way,
near Glastonbury and Somerton ; the other place is variously, and
very corruptly written : once "Seacescet." But there is still better
evidence that at this time the supremacy of Æthelbald of Mercia
was acknowledged in this district of Wessex. A charter, also
dated A.D. 744, of a gift of land at "Baldheresberge et Scobbanuuirthe "—Baltonsburg and, as some say, Shapwick—to Glastonbury, by a lady called Lulla, with the licence of Æthelbald, "qui
Britannicæ insulæ monarchiam dispensat." The first signature is
Æthelbald's, followed by Cuthred of Wessex "annuens ;" after
which other witnesses, including Herewald, Bishop of Sherborne.
It is printed in the Monasticon[2] and by Mr. Kemble,[3] both from
the same manuscript, but with many slight variations in orthography which seem to be arbitrary in either. Mr. Kemble prints
"Hilla," but John of Glastonbury has "Lulla," and so have both
Dugdale and the new Monasticon. Mr. Kemble puts his star stigma
but, although not of contemporary clerkships, it must transmit, in
substance, a more ancient deed, and is at least an accumulative
ancient and written confirmation of the external evidence already
given of the supremacy of Mercia in this part of Wessex, and the
subordination of Cuthred, even within the territory allotted to him
at the contest of A.D. 741. Observe, in passing, an example, in the
name "Scobbanuuirthe," of the Mercian—" uuerdin "—in a
transition form towards the "-worthy " of North Devon.

At all events, it is not to be wondered at that we should find
a St. Cuthbert on the north coast of Cornwall, among the other
symptoms that have been given of a Mercian settlement there.
But one in Devon deserves some particular notice ; because it is
found identified with one of the examples of "-worthy " which
is an outlier, and far away from the crowd that has been so much
dwelt upon. These two tests of Mercian influence have indeed
travelled far away from their fellows, but travelled together. It

---

[1] Page 105.   [2] 1846. Glaston. No. LXXXV.   [3] Cod. Dip., No. XCII.

is at Widworthy, in the eastern corner of the county, between
Honiton and Axminster, where the dedication and the termination,
although compatriots, are both strangers together. No chronicle
explains this, though no doubt it has a story never yet written.
But it seems cruel to forsake the St. Cuthbert at Wells to account
for itself, unhelped. After all that has been lately said, and insisted
upon, to the contrary, what if it should turn out that the " Sumer·
tun " of the Annal of A.D. 733, was Somerton in Somersetshire,
twelve miles south of Wells, as our deprecated obsolete school-
books used to teach us ? Another twenty-five miles reaches Widworthy. The then existing Foss-Way, which, even in its grass-grown
abandoned fragments, is still a broad and practicable travelling road,
passes within a very few miles of Wells, Glastonbury, Somerton,
and Widworthy.

But a more substantial evidence, of a long continuance of
Mercian influence beyond the Tamar, is not wanting : and even of
its great extension farther westward, down to the time of King
Alfred. A large hoard of coins and gold and silver ornaments
was found near St. Austell in 1774 ; and a description and tabu-
lation was lately published, by Mr. Rashleigh of Menabilly, of
114 coins that were rescued from the scramble.[1] Of these, no less
than 60 were of Mercian Kings (A.D. 757-874), whilst only seven·
teen belong to the then dominant West-Saxon sole monarchs (A.D.
800 to Alfred), and one to Northumbria.

Add to these notes of the Anglian —and not Saxon—kinship
of the English population of north-east Cornwall, the recurrence in
that county of what, to uncritical ears, has a great likeness to the
song or musical cadence already mentioned as met with in Mercia
proper. West Saxons who had seen the first production of the
comedy of " John Bull," used to tell us with much relish, how this
peculiarity was imitated upon the stage : and, in spite of the
friction of an active scholastic career, it is still occasionally dis·
cernible in cathedral pulpits. It has even maintained, to recent
times, a feeling among the West Saxons of Devon that a Cornishman

------

[1] An account of A.S. Coins, &c. Communicated to the Numismatic
Society of London, by Jonathan Rashleigh, Esq., 1868.

is, in some degree, a foreigner. What again about the "Cornish hug" in wrestling?[1] so strongly contrasted with the hold-off grip of the collar or shoulders, and the "fair back-fall" which is the pride of the Devonshire champion. It has nothing to do with the erudite difference of Celt and Teuton. The men of Devon—such as Drake and Raleigh[2]—have nearly as much Celtic blood as those of Cornwall. Cornishmen are fond of saying that their English speech is more correct than that of Devon : by which they mean, that their dialect is nearer to the one that has had the luck to run into printed books. Perhaps it is more Anglian and less Saxon. After a neighbourship of nearly twelve hundred years, let them now shake hands and be Anglo-Saxons : or Englishmen, if they prefer it, and wish to include the super-critics in their greeting.

Five out of the six extraneous dedications of St. Werburgh have now been referred to the active presence of Æthelbald, at the places where they are found, especially in connection with his exploits as they are obscurely recorded in the two Anglo-Saxon Annals of the years 741 and 743. The sixth, and last, of them remains, in like manner, to be brought into contact with him, and with the other recited Annal of the intermediate year, 742. We left three of the dedications as sentinels of their founder's conquest of his southern frontier of Wiccia. Two more were at the more distant duty, of keeping guard over his strategic settlement, on the western rear of Wessex. The one yet to be dealt with is that of a church still known by the name of that saint, yet more distant from her Mercian home ; in the extreme south-eastern county of Kent : and it only remains to enquire what business it has had ; not only so far away from its midland cradle, but also from the abiding places of its fellow wanderers.

Perhaps this would have been a much shorter task than either of the others, but that, at this part of the enquiry, our path is crossed by a controversy that began nearly three centuries ago, and has been ever since maintained with more or less warmth ; and with so much learning, and variety of opinion, that the only

---

[1] *Wessexonicè* " vvrasseling."

[2] No matter about their names. Their ethnical pedigree is distinctly blazoned in their portraits.

point of approach to unanimity among the contenders seems to be
an acknowledgment that they have each left it unsettled. Yet
this includes the question before us ; whether or not the Annal 742
of the Chronicle really concerns that part of the island wherein
the last of our outlying series of St. Werburghs has come to our
hands. It is, indeed, believed that the newly-imported fact itself,
of our finding this dedication where it is, may be a weighty contri-
bution to the settlement of the question ; yet the controversy has
been so long carried on, and has involved so great an array of
authoritative and orthodox scholarship ; that we can only presume
to pass it, by carefully and respectfully over-climbing it, and not
by a contemptuous Remusian leap.

This remaining sixth St. Werburgh is situated within that
small peninsula of the north shore of Kent, which is insulated by
the mouths of the Thames and Medway. In fact, it is not unlike a
tongue in a mouth, of which Essex and the Isle of Sheppey are as
the teeth or gums. A line from Rochester bridge to Gravesend
would separate more than the entire district from the mainland :
indeed it is all of the county of Kent that is north of Rochester.
It consists of an elevated chalk promontory, about ten or twelve
miles from east to west, and four from north to south, inclosing
several small fertile valleys : added to which, on the north or
Thames front, is a broad alluvial level or marsh, within the
estuary of that river, of several miles in width. Camden says of
this peninsula, " HO enim vocatur illa quasi Chersonessus." It
is, accordingly, a large specimen of that sort of configuration of a
tract of land in its relation to water, of which the name is often
found to contain the descriptive syllable, "-holm," "-ham," or
"-hoe." Whether or not these three are dialectic varieties of one
word, need not here be considered : it is certain, however, that
the names of such peninsular tracts are very often found to be
marked with "-hoe ; " and " Hoo "[1] is the name of the hundred

---

[1] A remarkable cluster of four or five names, with the form "-hoe,"
occurs on the coast of North Devon, in that part where we have already
pointed to the unrecorded Mercian descents upon the Damnonian Britons
(see before pp. 119-121). This is very faraway from the much more numerous
assemblages of it, which are in the Anglian parts of England. It has been

which still constitutes the largest and most prominent portion of this peninsula. So it was already called, even before the early time with which we shall find our own concern with it ; for in a charter, dated A.D. 738,[1] it is already mentioned as "regio quæ vocatur Hohg." In the Anglo-Saxon Chronicle, A D. 902, it is mentioned as "Holme." In Domesday,[2] the hundred which constitutes the peninsular portion, is called "*HOV*;" the isthmus portion having already, however, become a separate hundred, then called "Essamele," now "Shamwell." The towns in the district have their proper names added to "Hoo," as "Hoo-St.·Mary," and "Hoo-St-Werburgh :" and this last has the church above referred to. This is situated on the southern or Medway shore of the Hoo ; but on the cliff of the northern side of the elevated core of the peninsula, and over-looking the great reach of the

contended that this name-form is a vestige of the Danes, and, on this North Devon coast, the Danes might quite as likely have left their mark, as the Mercians. But one of them, "Martinhoe," is formed by the addition of "-hoe" to the christian dedication of the church : not likely, therefore, to have been named by a pagan colony. Another place, in East Devon not many miles from the Mercian Widworthy-St. Cuthbert already mentioned, (p. 125), called "Pinhoe," is recorded in the Anglo-Saxon Chronicle, A.D. 1001, to have been burnt *by* the Danes in revenge of a Saxon defeat. Would this revenge have fallen upon their own countrymen? Also, close to the South Devon dedication of St. Werburgh (p. 121), at Wembury, before mentioned, are two examples of this name-form. One, the well-known "Hoe," of Plymouth ; another, the village of "Hooe," in the promontory itself, where Wembury stands. Again, we have seen above that this very "regio," in Kent, which now engages us, was so named "Hogh" so early as A.D. 738. Very early for the Danes. Add to this : contemporary with the first appearance of the Danes in Northumbria, at Lindisfarne, there was already a place called "Billingahoh," now "Billing*ham*," near Stockton.

It is, therefore, evident that "-hoe" was here before the Danes, and can be no other than an Anglian peculiarity. It is, therefore, an additional evidence, and very strong confirmation, of what has been already said of the great Mercian descent upon Devon, that this Anglianism is found strewed in the very path of it.

It will presently be seen that, besides Simeon of Durham, and other early chroniclers, both Somner and Camden took it for granted that "-hoe" is only another form, or dialect of "-ham." It is however not unlikely, that, as in many other cases, a second mark of names "-haw" or "-haugh," said to be Danish, has been concurrent with and undistinguished from this.

[1] Cod. Dip., No. LXXXV.

[2] 8*b*.

estuary of the Thames, and the broad alluvial level embraced by
it, is the town of "Cliffe;" of which the church has the dedication St. Helen. The two churches are just four miles apart.
There are several other churches now in the peninsula, but the
others have been attributed to these two, of St. Werburgh and
St. Helen, as their mother churches, of which the other parishes
are ancient offshoots or chapelries.

Among the most famous names of places in England, during the
long aggressive reigns of Æthelbald and Offa, when, for the largest
part of the eighth century, the other kingdoms were more or less
threatened with the supremacy of Mercia, was that of a place
called Cloveshoe or Clovesham.[1] Its celebrity has been, no doubt,
much enhanced by its intimate connection with the Church
History of that period; but it has shared, with many of the names
of the localities of the most important events of the history of
those times, in a great deal of uncertainty and controversy as to
the actual place.

Few monuments of those ages are preserved to us in such
multitude as names of places, and in such apparent entireness;
but few are of such uncertain and doubtful appropriation. Although we are living in the midst of the scenes of the greatest
events of our early history; yet one of the most surprising
circumstances is, that of the number of the names of the places
that have remained almost unaltered, during the interval of
twelve centuries, so few of them can, with any degreee of
certainty, be identified: so that, although a Gazetteer or Index Locorum of those times would be a most valuable help
it would be the most difficult to compile; and, judging from past
attempts at contributions to it, impossible to be done with any
reasonable approach to trustworthiness. The visible monuments
have almost entirely been swept from off the face of the earth.
Towns, then of importance and even magnitude, if not now
entirely subject to the plough, are only represented by the merest
villages; and religious institutions have had their identity drowned

[1] First mentioned by Beda as " Clofeshoch," and in K. Alfred's
translation " Clofeshooh."

by the importation of later monastic orders; and generally by more catholic, but less national or local, dedications. The names of the places, in some few cases identified by immemorial traditions, are often the only indications of the whereabouts of some of the greatest events; but even the names themselves are obscured by the different methods, used in that age and in ours, of distinguishing them from other similar names; and the traditions, which should have preserved them, are interrupted by the long interval, between the events themselves, and the time at which the names first come again into our sight.

But this Clovesho = Clofeshoum = or Clobesham [1] had necessarily retained its hold upon the public memory of the ages from the eighth to the sixteenth centuries, from the importance to the Church of the great acts of councils, both royal and pontifical, there held; and the memory or tradition of the National Church, was, of all others, the most vivid and tenacious of any, during that long period · perhaps the only one which may be said to have bridged it, unbroken by interruptions, such as dynastic revolutions. When the tradition of the actual whereabouts of this famous place comes first into our view, we find it attached to the "Hoo" of Kent above described, and to the place called "Cliffe" there situated. The name now current is "Cliffe-at-Hoo," and this appears to have been the form in which it came to Camden's knowledge: at any rate, in the earlier editions of Britannia (1587), he mentions this place as "Clives at Ho Bedæ dictum."

There is, however, extant a still earlier record, that the tradition had not yet been doubted by the learned. The Rev. Prebendary Earle, Professor of Anglo-Saxon at Oxford, has most judiciously preserved some marginal notes of the 16th century, that he found in that MS. of the Saxon Chronicle,[2] which he distinguishes as "C.;" which notes he considers to be "written in an Elizabethan hand:" but as will be presently seen they must have been of the reign of Henry VIII. One of these is written in the margin against one of the occurrences of the name "Clofes hoo" · in the Chronicle, and reads "doctor Hethe's benyffyce;" and

[1] See Cod. Dip. passim, for other varieties of the name.
[2] Two S. Chronicles, Oxford, 1565.

Mr. Earle asks, "where may Dr. Hethe's benefice have been?"[1] To this question of the Professor's, two more may be added : Who was Dr. Hethe? And who was—evidently his intimate acquaintance—the writer of the marginal notes to the Chronicle?

The answers to these three questions will shew what sort of men these were whom we find in possession of this historical tradition concerning the actual place of those famous synods ; and who, long before any question about it had been raised, by the incipient critical scepticism of the 17th century, out of fancied probabilities, are here seen treating it as an undoubted fact. These answers will also shew what advantages, of time and local associations, they had for judgment of the fact.

The benefice, then, was the Rectory of the Cliffe above mentioned, situated in the peninsula, or Hoo, north of Rochester. This living was held, from 1543 to 1548, by Dr. Nicholas Heath :

[1] It is to be regretted that editors of ancient texts, have not more generally extended their care to the preservation of marginal and other adventitious notes, even when they are of comparatively much later date than the texts, which of course are their chief care. Such valuable fragments are in imminent peril at the present day ; for whenever a new discovery of ancient books or records is now brought to the notice of the most distinguished experts, the very first piece of advice is that they shall be "cleaned," "repaired," and "skilfully" rebound. See, among others, examples in the Historical Manuscripts Commission, *passim*. Why the binding, and even the *status quo* itself, is a part of the essence of such things, as monuments. But manuscripts, with far less excuse, are following the churches on the broad way to refaction, as it may be mildly called.

When the fanciers of books, especially in London, as well as experts in manuscripts, make a fortunate acquisition of anything, both fine and unique ; after the usual notes of admiration, such as "truly marvellous," etc., they go on to say, "but it deserves a better jacket." And at once order it to be stripped of its monumental covering, and scoured of the autumnal tints of many ages ; its pedigree, contained in ancient shelf-marks, and autographs, is discarded ; often valuable notarial records of events that have for safety, like monuments in churches, been entered on the covers and fly-leaves, are lost ; and it is finally converted into a monument of nineteenth century skill in smooth morocco, "antique style," &c All that is really wanted, however, is either a box-case, or other apparatus for protection. Keep charters or papers nearly as you do Bank of England Notes. These are never bound for safe-keeping. On the outsides of these unattached bindings, or other provisions for safe-keeping, can be lavished whatever munificence, or luxury of modern art, may be thought to be a sufficient tribute of admiration to the object contained.

it was, therefore, during these years that the marginal notes were written. He was afterwards Bishop of Rochester, and of Worcester, and Archbishop of York, and Lord Chancellor ; and during the reign of Henry VIII, and to the accession of Elizabeth, took leading parts in most affairs, both in Church and State. Wood calls him "a most wise and learned Man, of great Policy, and of as great Integrity."

As to Dr. Heath's friend, the writer of the marginal notes, there can be no doubt that he was Dr. Nicholas Wotton : one of the small knot of revivers of Anglo-Saxon literature, and of those, named by Mr. Earle,[1] as a few persons who then had the handling of Saxon MSS. It is found that the long active and distinguished career, of each of these two men, ran both in the same groove :— through the same period, in the same rank and line of affairs, and locally together.[2] They were both part authors of the well-known Institution of a Christian Man, 1537. Wotton was the first Dean of Canterbury, and so continued for more than twenty-five years : also Dean of York. During two intervals he administered, by commission, the Province of Canterbury ; and was named, along with Parker, as successor to that Primacy.

These are the two men, who are first found in possession of the historical tradition, that the famous place where the Mercian kings, with the Archbishops, the Bishop of Rochester, and the Mercian and other Bishops, held their councils; the acts of which must, in all ages, have been most conspicuous to learned English Canonists, was no other than this very Cliffe-at-Hoo ; and it is evident, from the directness of the marginal note, that they held it as an unquestioned fact. So, about fifty years afterwards, when he published Britannia, it was as we have seen, also without reserve, accepted by Camden.[3] Up to this time the tradition—not among men who accept Geoffrey of Monmouth's stories and the like, but among the learned—was yet undisturbed. But twenty years later we find Camden wavering ; influenced only by speculations on the

---

[1] Introd. LXVIII.

[2] See Strype's Works *passim*, where above 100 transactions of Heath are referred to, and above 50 of Wotton.

[3] Edn. 1587, p. 196.

nature of the district, and a then prevalent distorted perspective
of the remote historical circumstances of the time concerned.   In
the edition of Britannia, which received his latest revision,[1] he
qualifies his former statement, by saying that he no longer dares
to affirm, as others do, whether or not the Cliffe in the little
country called Ho, may be the "Cliues at Ho," so celebrated
in the infancy of the Anglican Church ; because the place seems
not to be a convenient one for holding the Synod ; and that the
actual place seems to have been within the kingdom of Mercia,
rather than Kent.   From that time to this present day the place,
indicated by this name, has ranked among the most disputed and
unsettled questions of early English topography.

It also happened, that Camden, when treating of Berkshire,
had quoted from the Chronicle of Abingdon, a passage which set
forth, that, before the abbey was founded at, or removed to, that
place, its name had been "Sheouesham," and was a royal residence.   This name, thus brought forward by Camden, struck the
fancy of Somner the learned compiler of the earliest Anglo-Saxon
Dictionary,[2] who, collating it with Camden's hesitation at the Cliffe-
at-Hoo tradition, thought he saw in " Sheouesham " a scriptorial
erroneous variation of " Clouesho or -ham ;" Abingdon being, in
accordance with the conception of the greater constancy of the
frontiers of the " Heptarchy " then prevalent, more likely to be the
place of councils, at which the Mercian kings so often presided.
And this seemed to be the more likely ; because the Abingdon
Chronicle also said, that Abingdon had hitherto been a royal residence, when the abbey was founded, from which it got its new
name.   The Abingdon Chronicle is, of course, good for its proper
uses, but where it says that "Seouescham civitas" had been a
"sedes regia," although the name has an English colouring, it is
evidently speaking of British or ante-Saxon times.   If a royal
residence during the reign of Æthelbald, it must have been of
the West Saxons, and not of the Mercians.   It could not, therefore, have been the Cloveshoe where Æthelbald presided.

If this liberty of interpretation should be permitted, it is

---

[1] 1607, folio.   [2] Oxon, 1659.

plain that it would be enough to shake almost any recorded name. Indeed another example of its use, if also tolerated, would reverse the one itself that had been proposed : would, if the other was enough to carry it to Abingdon, be strong enough to bring it back again to Hoo. In the charter, dated A.D. 738,[1] four years before the earliest recorded Cloveshoe Council, a piece of land is called "Andscohesham." This is certainly within the very Hoo district itself, which is the site of the Cloveshoe of the tradition ; being described as "in regione quæ nocatur Hohg." Mr. Kemble prints the charter from the Textus Roffensis, but omits the title or endorsement that fixes the very spot in the Hoo that it refers to. This is, however, preserved in Monasticon Anglicanum :[2] " De Stokes, que antiquitus vocabatur Andscohesham ;" and Stoke is now a parish in the Hoo, and close to Cliffe. There can be no doubt that the " And-" stands for, or is a corrupt reading of, " aed-" or the preposition " æt,-" so continually carried, along with vernacular Anglo-Saxon names, into Latin documents ; and the name of this " Scohesham " of the Kentish Hoo would thus be practically identical with that of the " Scheouesham "— also written " Scuckesham "[3]—the alleged ancient name of Abingdon. Not that it is intended here to say that " Andscohesham " is a corruption of " Clovesham," although it would have been just as reasonable as Somner's inference ; but that Somner's conjecture for removing the place, might be retorted by one equally efficient to bring it back again. But even this might be worth farther scrutiny : for if this identity, of " Andscohesham " and " Clovesham," should prove to be the case, the ancient controversy would be determined at once, without the further trouble here being bestowed. This Andscohesham or Stoke is close also to Hoo-St.-Werburgh, and probably identical with " Godgcocesham," the place where " Eanmundus rex," or Eahlmund (= Alcmund, father of Egbert of Wessex) was living, when he added his form of approval to a gift,[4] of land at Islingham also close adjoining, by his co-rex of Kent, Sigered, to Earduulf Bishop of Rochester, (A.D. 759-765.)

---

[1] Cod. Dip., No. LXXXV.   [2] Rochester, Num. IV.

[3] Chron. of Abingdon.   [4] Cod. D., No. CXIV.

The likeness of the name Clovesho and Cliff-at-Hoo, is not of a
sort likely to suggest identity, except first prompted externally,
such as by an actual independent tradition; but after having
been thus brought together by external evidence, the structure
of the old name can thoroughly justify the identity.

But, however slender may have been this original philological
cause of disturbance, it served to carry the question, of the actual
place, out into the expansive region of conjecture; where it
has been ever since rolling and rebounding, from one end of the
land to the other, from that time to this.   Every succeeding
writer treating the matter as if it had been commissioned to him
to choose the place of the synods, according to his own views of
the fitness of things.   Bishop Gibson first accepted Somner's
conjecture, and so adopting Abingdon, concludes that "no sane
man," who admits the authority of the Abingdon Chronicle, " can
stick at it:"[1] the Abingdon Chronicle having never said it except
through Somner's distortion.   Smith's gloss, on the name in Beda
is, " Vulgo Cliff, juxta Hrofes caester."   But he continues, in a
note, that Somner's opinion in preferring Abingdon seems not
unworthy of observation.   He recites Camden, but concludes,
" Sed in his nihil ultra conjecturam, & illam certe valde fluctuan-
tem."[2]   A conclusion which is even prophetic.   In Dr. Geo. Smith's
map to Beda it is, however, placed at Abingdon.   Smith's note is
transcribed as it stands by Wilkins;[3] and again by Sir T. D.
Hardy.[4]

Capt. John Stevens, in a note in his translation of Bede,
(A.D. 1723,) says, as to the true place being Cliffe, "Of this
opinion are the two great antiquarians, Spelman and Talbot, to
which Lambard likewise gives in, though with caution."   This
must be Dr. Robert Talbot, Canon of Norwich, another early
Saxon scholar, reign Henry VIII., who left transcripts of charters
of Abingdon,[5] and is, therefore, another early learned witness of
the tradition.   Spelman's interpretation is " Cloveshoviæ (vulgo

[1] Chron. Sax. Oxon. 1692.   [2] Bæda H. E., cura Jo. Smith, Cant.
722, p. 1748.   [3] Concilia, I., 161.   [4] Monumenta Hist. Brit.
Tanner Bibl. Brit., p. 703.

Clyff)."[1] The Rev. Joseph Stevenson[2] recites the option of Cliffe and Abingdon. Of the church historians, Fuller remonstrates against Camden's doubts, with his usual moderation. Collier merely calls it " Clovesho, or Clyff, near Rochester."

By this time the Abingdon speculation had become strong enough to carry double : to be able to be called in to the help of other theories, on outside matters. The ingenious Welsh philologer, William Baxter,[3] gets from it an offspring *ergo*. He makes Abingdon the " Caleva Attrebatum," *because* it had been " Clovesho :" upon which, by a sort of "To-my-love and from-my-love " formula, Dr. W. Thomas[4] completes the symmetry of a logical circle, by citing " Calleva Attrebatum" as evidence that Cloveshoe is near Henley-on-Thames, then thought to be Calleva.

R. Gough, in Additions to Camden, leaves it at Abingdon on Bp. Gibson's argument : and, throughout the eighteenth century, Abingdon seems to have been favoured ; the writers being much given to copy each other. Dr. Lingard, 1803, quoting Capt. Stevens's translation of Bede, says "probably Abingdon," and so also puts it in his Anglo-Saxon map ; but Capt. Stevens had only quoted both views, without adopting either.

The later editors of the Saxon Chronicle, Dr. Ingram and Mr. Thorpe, return to the tradition, contenting themselves with the simple gloss " Cliff-at-Hoo, Kent," " Cliff near Rochester." Miss Gurney, however, prudently says, " Cliff in Kent, or Abingdon." Professor Earle gives the valuable note and question about Dr. Heath, before mentioned, but leaves the main question, of the place, open. On the other hand, the Dictionaries, since Somner : Lye says "fortasse Abbingdon," and Dr. Bosworth follows with " perhaps Abingdon," quoting both Somner and Lye.

But the nineteenth century took a fresh stride away from the start of the seventeenth. Whilst accepting from the eighteenth the inheritance of the doubt, it next renounced the claim itself for which the doubt had been raised. It is no longer Abingdon, but wherever it may be thought likely—Dr. Lappenberg[5] places it in Oxfordshire ;

---

[1] Concilia, 1639, p. 242.   [2] Beda, 1838, p. 200.   [3] Gloss. Ant. Brit., 1733.   [4] Account of Worc. Cath., 1736, p. 120.   [5] A.S.K., 1 225.

D

Mr. N. E. S. A. Hamilton[1] "co. Berks." Mr. Kemble more boldly carries it to "the hundred of Westminster, and county of Gloucester, perhaps near Tewksbury."[2] Next year,[3] he more firmly says "Doubts have been lavished upon the situation of this place, which I do not share," and concludes that it was "not far from Deerhurst, Tewksbury, and Bishop's Cleeve; not at all improbably in Tewksbury itself, which may have been called Clofeshoas, before the erection of a noble abbey at a later period gave it the name it now bears."

Messrs. Haddan and Stubbs[4] accept the objections of their forerunners against Cliff-at-Hoo, thinking that this place "rests solely on the resemblance of the name." They say of the Abingdon = Sheovesham theory, that it is also "the merest conjecture." They also reject Mr. Kemble's Tewkesbury as founded on a mistaken identity of Westminster hundred with another place sometimes called "Westminster," in the Mercian charters, (A.D. 804-824). This is, indeed, Westbury-on-Trym. But why was the minster there called "west," and where was the minster that was east of it? At an earlier date (A.D. 794) it had already got its present name, "Uuestburg." Messrs. Haddan and Stubbs leave the question of the true place of Cloveshoe as they find it, neither endorsing the original tradition, nor indulging in the freedom of choice which had been established for them. In another work,[5] however, Mr. Haddan has said, "On the locality of Cloveshoo itself, unfortunately, we can throw no more light than may be contained in the observation, that St. Boniface invariably styles the English synod, 'Synodus *Londinensis*;' and that . . . . . the immediate vicinity of that city—in all other respects the most probable of all localities—seems consequently the place where antiquarians must hunt for traces of the lost Cloveshoo." How far Cliffe, situated near the mouth of the Thames, may satisfy or contradict the "Londinensis" of S. Bonifatius must be left to be judged. Dean Hook recites his fore-goers, but not quite understanding them :—"Where Cloveshoo was it is impossible to say,

[1] Will. Malm., G. P. 1870.   [2] Cod. Dip., 1848.   [3] Saxons in E., 1849, I, 191. The *name* of Tewkesbury is, however, appparently older than even this ancient monastery.   [4] Councils, Vol. III., Oxf., 1871, p. 122.   [5] Remains, p. 326.

some antiquarians placing it at Cliff-at-Hoo, in Kent ; some in the
neighbourhood of Rochester ; others contending for Abingdon ;
others again for Tewkesbury."[1] But Cliff-at-Hoo in Kent *is* in
the *near* neighbourhood of Rochester. The present state of the
question, therefore, seems to be, that it is given up as hopeless.

But the most strenuous renunciator of the Kentish tradition,
in favour of the Berkshire conjecture, was a learned and distinguished native of the Kentish locality itself : the Rev. John
Johnson. He is usually reckoned among the learned and suffering
body of the Nonjurors, but, by personal merits and some con-
cessions, he appears to have escaped their political ordeal ; having
retained his preferments throughout a long life. He is commonly
distinguished, from the other Johnsons of literature, as "Johnson
of Cranbrook." His remarks deserve all the more careful consideration, because he was born at Frindsbury, immediately adjoining
Cliffe, and the intermediate parish between it and Rochester. At
Frindsbury, in fact, was the "Aeslingham" of the Textus Roffensis, in one of the charters that concern the Hoo and the locality
now in question. He printed a Collection of Canons of the
English Church, in 1720.[2] In his preface and notes to the Synod
at which was ratified the submission of the usurped primacy of
Lichfield to that of Canterbury, A.D. 803, which is one of those
held at "clofeshoas ;"[3] he oddly brings it, as an argument that
Abingdon was the place, that the triumphant Archbishop of
Canterbury "was willing to meet" his reconciled insubordinate
rival, half way between Lichfield and Canterbury. Converting
what is a very strong presumption against Abingdon, into an act
of extreme humility on the part of the Archbishop. The learned
writer must have felt the difficulty, which he thus strove so hard to
liquidate into a virtue. After this, he goes on to allege that "there
is not a more unhealthy spot in the whole province, I may say in
all Christendom," than this district of the Hoo. With deference,
however, to such a writer, and a native of the spot, this account
of it does, to a mere visitor, seem to be exaggerated. The Gads-

[1] A-B. C., I., 224.   [2] New edition, by Rev. J. Baron, Oxford, 1850.
[3] C.D. CLXXXV.

D 2

Hill, of Falstaff, will bring the neighbourhood to the remembrance of many; and it has become more widely known of late years, by the last residence of another great master of humour and fiction, which is less than four miles from the church of Cliffe, and the outlook from which would be about identical with that from any Mercian Villa Regia that may have existed here. An ungrateful remembrance of the inflictions of schoolmasters, or other childish griefs, is often observed to haunt the later career of those to whose distinguished position they may have contributed.

In his "Addenda," Johnson afterwards says, "I find some worthy gentlemen still of opinion, that Cliff......was not unhealthy in the age of the Councils:" and he truly quotes charters from the Textus Roffensis, to show that the northern marshes, or levels, then already existed; and he urges that it "was, therefore, altogether unfit for a stated place of synod." That "As Cliff in Hoo was never a place of great note itself, so it lies, and ever did lie, out of the road to any place of note;" and he goes on to recite Somner and Camden's plea of the greater likelihood of Abingdon, for synods limited to the times of Mercian domination.

But the marshes are not in question, they are but an appendage to the Hoo. This peninsula is formed of a large fragment of the chalk at the eastern end of the North Kentish downs, called by geologists an "inlier" into the Thames basin; upon the heights, and in the valleys, of which the places concerned in this enquiry were situated. The marshes are a broad fringe of level pasture land,[1] advanced into the Thames estuary, beyond its north chalk cliff. In Kent the word "marsh" signifies the same as "more" in Somersetshire: which, although even Dr. Jamieson confounds the two, is a totally different word and thing, from the "muir," or "moor," for waste lands of a highland character. It is to such land as this that we owe the dairies of Cheddar; and if this objection should be good, Glastonbury and Wells, not to mention Ely and Croyland, must resign their venerable places in history. A very similar projection of alluvial level pasture extends

---

[1] "Bercaria" is a synonym for the East Marsh at Cliffe.—Monasticon Angl. V.I., p. 177, No. 52.

from Henbury and Shirehampton to the Bristol Channel, without disparagement of their salubrity. Mr. Johnson, having suffered much in health by a residence of a year or two at Appledore, in Kent, obtained the vicarage of Cranbrook, where he lived for eighteen years. It is likely that he was sensitive of climatal influences, and shy of those breezes that reach this island after passing over the great plains of central Europe : a tenderness, which neither Æthelbald nor Offa can be supposed to have shared with him.

It is plain, however, that this broad alluvial margin, extending from the northern edge of the heights, which are the substantial constituents of the Hoo peninsula, already existed, A.D. 779, at least a very large extent of it; for the first charter, so dated,[1] describes it as then "habentem quasi quinquaginta iugerum." In a later charter, A.D. 789,[2] the name of the projecting level appears as " Scaga."[3] It must already have become land of value to be granted in these charters ; and its identity is certain from the limits—Yantlet ("Jaenlade") water to "Bromgeheg," now " Bromey," on the higher land at Cooling. Does not the word "jugeru," used in the charter, indicate that this " marsh " was already cultivated or pasture land ? How it had been originally caused is, however, not hard to discern. It is, evidently, a large portion of the delta of the Thames, intercepted by the confluence of the other great river, the Medway, and thrown back behind the chalk promontory of the Hoo. Inside, and westward of this deposit, the tidal estuary makes a bold reach southward ; sweeping the western side of this level, and approaching the heights, so as, at Cliffe, Higham, and Chalk, to leave only a comparatively narrow fringe of level ; and it is on the heights at the southern bend of this reach, that are situated these three villages, which will presently be found, it is thought, to be interesting to us.

As to the most substantial objection, which of course has continued to be a constantly recurring ingredient of this contro-

---

[1] Cod. D. cxxxv.   [2] Cod. D. clvii.

[3] See Cleasby and Vigfusson, v. " Skaga." The northern pagans, afterwards such pests of Rochester, must have already landed here.

versy, that the place of the synods must have been within the
kingdom of Mercia, it seems a little oblique of the mark aimed at.
They were royal councils, and these must be expected to have
followed the presence of the king and his court, as was the case in
much later times than those now under consideration.   Most of
the remaining records of these synods at Cloveshoe, and of the
other national ones during the same period, show the king to have
presided ; and it is true that it is the Mercian King, who is so
found, during both of the long reigns of Æthelbald and Offa ; and
throughout the time of the domination of the Mercians in Kent.
The policy of the Mercian aggressors, during their long continued
contention for empire, to grasp the great estuaries of the island,
has already been referred to, and a glance at sheets I. and VI. of
the Ordinance survey will show how desirable was this Chersonesus
for the head quarters of a power, which made a chief point of the
possession of the Thames, and its only less valuable and smaller
sister, the Medway.   The opposite coast of the East Saxons had
already, for several reigns, been subjected to Mercia.   A.D. 704,
Suebræd, the regulus of the East Saxons, could not grant lands at
Twickenham, then in Essex, but " in᾽ prouincia quæ nuncupatur
middelseaxan," to Waldhere, Bishop of London, except " cum
licentia Æthelredi regis" of Mercia.[1]   Kent, less fortunate, was
still contended for by both Wessex and Mercia, as well as by
Sussex, and by all three it was successively ravaged ; and it even
looks as if the three contending invaders maintained, as clients,
rival pretenders, as kings of the parts of Kent at the time under
their power.   The division of Kent into Lathes may be a so-to-
speak fossil, or rather an archaic autograph upon the surface of
the county, of this state of it.   It is, however, certain that Mercia
ultimately made good a permanent domination of Kent ; and the
kings of Kent acknowledged that supremacy in their government,
by merely counter-subscribing the acts of the kings of Mercia.[2]

The mass of chalk, of which the body of the Hoo consists, is
said to pass under the Thames ; and a small continuation of it re-

[1] Cod. D., No. LII.

[2] For example, Cod. D. No. CXI., which grants lands in the Hoo itself,
viz. : Islingham in Frindsbury, adjoining Cliffe, to Rochester Cathedral.

appears on the Essex side, directly opposite Cliffe and Higham and
Chalk, at East Tilbury ; and having continued four miles westward,
behind the marsh marked by Tilbury Fort, dies out at Purfleet.[1] It
forms an elevated promontory at East Tilbury, penetrating the levels
on that side to the river. The present chief traject of the river is
about three miles westward, from Gravesend to the fort : but the
chalk promontory is the terminus of an ancient straight chain of
roads, which, although in some places interrupted by later breaks
and divergencies, indicates a traffic of ages, from this terminus on
the river, in a north-western direction, striking the Iknield Street
at Brentwood, and apparently afterwards still continuing the
same line : probably to Watling Street ; any rate to the heart of
the Mercian dominions : say, to Hertford, if you like.

There are various other substantial evidences of great ancient
intercourse of Essex with the Hoo of Kent, by a trajectus at this
place, between East Tilbury and Higham ; and Higham is only five
miles from Rochester bridge, by which the Watling Street entered
that city. Morant says, of the manor of Southall in East Tilbury,
" This estate goes now to the repair of Rochester bridge : when and
by whom given we do not find." [2] He also mentions the " famous
Higham Causeway " in connection with Tilbury.[3] Until the
reign of Stephen, the church at Higham had belonged to the
Abbot and Convents of St. John, Colchester.[4] The importance of
this Essex traject to the kingdoms north of the Thames, when
the domination of Mercia in Essex and Kent was beginning, may
be inferred from the fact that one of the two colleges, or capitular
churches, founded by Cedda, A.D. 653, in Essex, was at Tilbury.[5]
There is a place called Chadwell by West Tilbury. Some years
later, A.D. 676, when Æthelred of Mercia first devastated Kent,
it is evident that he used this passage ; for the destruction of
Rochester, five miles south of Higham and Cliffe, is the only one
of his exploits, on that expedition, specified by name.[6] So late as
A.D. 1203, Giraldus Cambrensis passed from Kent to Essex by
Tilbury. These incidents, connecting Tilbury and Higham, may

---

[1] Geol. Surv. of E. & W., vol. IV., London Basin, 1872, pp. 34, 35.
[2] H. of Essex, I., 235.   [3] P. 236.   [4] Mon. Anglic. Lillechurch (alias
Higham), Nos. IV. and V.   [5] Beda, H. E. III., 22.   [6] Beda, H. E., IV., 12,

qualify the surprise that has hitherto troubled church historians at finding that "Clofeshoch," at so early a date as A.D. 673, was appointed, at "Herutford," as the place for future councils, even if Herutford had been Hertford, as some say.

The conclusion that the line of approach, and of the first invasion of Kent by the Mercians, was by a passage from the Essex coast to Higham or Cliffe; and that the peninsula of Hoo, adjoining Rochester, had then and long after been the basis of their domination of that kingdom; had been already formed, from what has been already said. And it was at this point, that it was thought worth while to see what the chief county historians say about the two termini of the trajectus.

This is Hasted's statement :—

"*Plautius*, the *Roman* General under the *Emperor Claudius*, in the year of Christ, 43, is said to have passed the river *Thames* from *Essex* into *Kent*, near the mouth of it, with his army, in pursuit of the flying *Britons* who being acquainted with the firm and fordable places of it passed it easily. (Dion. Cass, lib. lx.) The place of this passage is, by many, supposed to have been from *East Tilbury*, in *Essex*, across the river to *Higham*. (By Dr. Thorpe, Dr. Plott, and others.) Between these places there was a *ferry* on the river for many ages after, the usual method of intercourse between the two counties of Kent and Essex for all these parts, and it continued so till the dissolution of the abbey here; before which time Higham was likewise the place for shipping and unshipping corn and goods in great quantities from this part of the country, to and from *London* and elsewhere. The probability of this having been a frequented ford or passage in the time of the *Romans*, is strengthened by the visible remains of a raised causeway or road, near 30 feet wide, leading from the *Thames* side through the marshes by *Higham south-ward* to this *Ridgway* above mentioned, and thence across the *London* highroad on *Gads-hill* to *Shorne-ridgway*, about half a-mile beyond which adjoins the *Roman Watling-street* road near the entrance into *Cobham-park*. In the pleas of the crown in the 21st year of K. Edward I., the *Prioress* of the nunnery of *Higham* was found liable to maintain a bridge and causeway that led from *Higham* down to the river *Thames*, in order to give the better and easier passage to such as would ferry from thence into Essex."[1]

It may be added that the Hoo peninsula has other marks of having been, at much earlier times, a district of great transit. There is, perhaps, no other part of England, of so small an extent, which has so many and clustered examples of "Street" in names of secluded spots—including the almost ubiquitous "Silver Street"[2]—quite disengaged from those that follow the line itself of Watling-street. Yet Mr. Johnson of Cranbrook goes on to say, " As Cliffe in Hoo was never a place of note itself, so it lies, and ever did lie, out of the road to any place of note." It is believed that he has greatly under-rated the substantial results of such a dynastic change as we are now considering; followed, for a thousand years, by its sequential changes on the material surface of the earth.

At all events, this was, evidently, the earliest line of approach, by which Mercia, with its contingents, the other Anglian nations and the East Saxons, whom it had either subdued or otherwise allied, invaded Kent; and this continued to be its chief or only access for some years. A single glance, at the geography of the Hoo, will show the value of such an advanced peninsula, as the basis of such an incursion upon the centre of Kent; and as the stronghold from which the subjection of that kingdom could be maintained. We have other means of knowing that it was probably, at least, thirty years before a second or optional approach was secured by way of the east of Kent. This second access must have been a much coveted one, and when it came into hand must have been of great value ; particularly in regard to the occasional, or at least frequent, royal residence already established at the Hoo. The Watling Street, the greatest and most frequented of

[1] Hist. Kent, I., p. 528.

[2] See Dr. J. H. Pring, in the Somerset Arch. Soc.

all the highways then existing, led from the very heart of Mercia, in a direct line through Middlesex, to the very isthmus of the peninsula itself.   Although Kent had been already invaded, A.D. 676, yet so late as A.D. 695,[1] London remained subject to Essex ; but, as we have already seen, only nine years afterwards Twickenham, in the province called "Middelseaxan," had become subject to Mercia.

Some of our most learned historians describe the "Middle Saxons" as a very small people, forming a part of the East Saxons ; but they are obliged to confess that they find very little to say about them.   It is believed that there never was a separate people called Middle Saxons.   They have been created out of a snatched analogy, of the mere name "Middlesex," with "Essex," "Sussex," and "Wessex."   There can be little doubt that Middlesex represents the original civitas, or territory, of the local government, of its urbs or burgh of London, the capital of the kingdom of Essex.   Like other great commercial seaports or staples, this already great mart had maintained much of the condition of a free city ; and, in passing, along with its territory from Essex to the ascendant power of Mercia, it may not have been by conquest, but by a voluntary exercise of that instinct, to unite in the fortunes of an advancing supremacy, which is often associated with, and perhaps closely allied to, commercial habits.   At all events, it is at this time that the name, Middlesex, first comes to light ;[2] and it is believed that instead of being, like the names of the Saxon nations, formed by the addition of an adjective ; the "middle" of this newer name is a preposition, and that it means, that Anglian acquisition which had now thrust itself *between* the East Saxons and the South and West Saxons.   The Anglo-Saxon Dictionaries produce an example, from one of the glossaries of Ælfric, of "Middel-gesculdru" = the space *between* the shoulders.

But although, in the existing records of the series of Councils and Synods that were held during the ascendancy of Mercia, and often presided over by the Mercian kings in person, the name of

---

[1] Cod. Dip., No. xxxviii.

[2] One copy of the A.-S. Chronicle has "Middelseaxe" as early as A.D. (53, the other four testify this to be miswritten for "Middelengle."

Cloveshoe is frequent, as the place of convention ; other places, as "Cealchythe" and "Acle," are also frequent and continuous. And the names of the councillors, who sign the acts as witnesses, have a certain current identity, with only such changes as may be expected by lapse of time, rather than of change of the region where the assemblies had been convened. After the king, usually follows the Archbishop of Canterbury ; then the Bishop of Lichfield, followed by the other Mercian Bishops ; and then of the other subject kingdoms.

These two places, Cealchythe and Acle, have been as great puzzles to enquirers as Clovesho itself ; and they also have been placed in very distant regions ; the sounds of their names being apparently thought to be the only consideration. Cealchythe was thought by Archbishop Parker to be in Northumbria ; but Alford said Chelsea ; Spelman that it was within the kingdom of Mercia. [1] Gibson suggests Culcheth in Lancashire, as although in Northumbria, not far from Mercia. Miss Gurney also says " Perhaps Kilcheth on the southern border of Lancashire." Dr. W. Thomas gives it to Henley-on-Thames, partly because he considered it "near" Cloveshoe ; Wilkins nor Kemble make any venture ; others, adopted by Messrs. Haddan and Stubbs, and, as far as the name alone would have settled it, with a very great deal of apparent reason, would have placed it at Chelsea. The ancient forms of the name of Chelsea, of which examples are by no means scarce, seem all directly to lead up to an identity with that of the councils. One of these, of the baptism, A.D. 1448, of John, son of Richard, Duke of York, recorded in Will. Wyrcester's Anecdota, is, for example, at " Chelchiethe." But the name of the council seems to resolve itself into " Chalk-hythe," and there is no chalk at Chelsea. But even this has been got over by taking the first portion of " Chelsey " for " chesil " or gravel ; and this favours the ancient forms of Chelsea = Chelchythe, rather more than it does the variations in the name of the council ; which on the whole lean towards " chalk " or " Chalkhythe." Dr. Ingram[2] adopts " Challock, or Chalk, in Kent ;" and Mr. Thorpe repeats that suggestion, with the addition of a " ? "

[1] Conc. pp. 291, 313, 314.   [2] A. Sax. Chron.

As to this " Chalk," it is also in the district of the Hoo, and
is the adjoining parish westward of Higham ; on the same chalk
ridge, whereon both Higham and Cliff-at-Hoo are situated. The
village is two miles west of Higham church, and all three
are practically the same place, within a space of four miles ; of
which the ancient trajectus above mentioned is at the centre. The
face of the cliff, upon which Cliffe stands, is still quarried for
chalk, which is shipped in a small creek that runs up to the cliff.
It will at once come to mind, how constantly such wharfs are
called " hythe," throughout the navigable portion of the Thames ;
and how frequently that word forms a part of the names of them.
That river has, indeed, almost—not quite—a monopoly of this
name-form. But the Ordnance Surveyors[1] show an eastward
detachment of Chalk parish, within half a mile of Higham church,
and close to that point of the shore which would have been the
hythe of the traject. There can be little doubt that this detachment is a survival of the " Chalkhythe " at which some of the
councils were dated, whilst others were at Cliffe-at-Hoo adjoining.
An endorsed confirmation,[2] under Coenulf, has the formula, " in
synodali conciliabulo *juxta* locum qui dicitur caelichyth."

Another frequent name, of the place of convention of some of
this series of councils during Mercian ascendancy, is " Acle " or
" Acleah," which has been as great a puzzle as the others. This
name may be expected to appear in any such modern forms as
Oakley, Okeley, Ockley, or Ackley, which are very numerous in
nearly every part of England ; indeed, wherever the oak has
grown : and rather a free use of this wide choice has been made
in the attempts to find the place of the councils so dated. The
most accepted one seems to be Ockley, south of Dorking, near the
confines of Surrey and Sussex ; apparently attracted by a battle
with the Danes there, A.D. 851. But this happened in later and
Wessexian times. Lambarde (about A.D. 1577) thought it likely
to be somewhere in the Deanery of Ackley, in Leicestershire :
Spelman, in the Bishopric of Durham. Dr. Ingram says, " Oakley
in Surrey." Professor Stubbs says of one act of Offa so dated that

---

[1] 6-inch scale.   [2] C.D., No. cxvi.

it " is unquestionably Ockley in Surrey," and affords " a strong presumption that the other councils of the southern province said to be at Acleah, were held at the same place," apparently because the charter before him is a grant to Chertsey. But the substance of these royal grants does not show the place where they were executed. They are the Acts of the Supreme Court of Appeal. Ingram and Thorpe give Ockley, Surrey. Miss Gurney, " Acley, Durham?" Kemble, "Oakley or Ackley, Kent, or Ockley, Surrey," Sir T. D. Hardy says "in Dunelmia;" no doubt adopting Spelman's judgment.

Turning again to the Ordnance Survey,[1] at one mile-and-a-half from the church at Cliff-at-Hoo, and rather nearer to it than Higham church itself, will be seen a building marked "Oakly;" or, in the six-inch scale, two: Oakley and Little Oakley. Reverting to Hasted's account of the parish of Higham,[2] we also find that it contained two manors, Great and Little Okeley; and he quotes the Book of Knight's Fees, K. John, where it is written, "Acle."[3] Oakley lies in the direct way from the ancient traject to Rochester bridge, and has been held liable to repair the fourth pier of it. In Domesday it appears as "Arclei." But the existence of this very place can be realised at a date eight years earlier than the first recorded Synod at Aclea. Mr. Kemble has printed[4] a grant of Offa, dated A.D. 774, to Jaenberht the Archbishop, of a piece of land in a place called "Hehham," now Higham; of which one portion is conterminous with Acleag—"per confinia acleage"—, another part touches "ad colling"—now Cooling with its Castle,—afterwards bounded by "mersctun," since Merston, and other lands "Sci andree," i.e. of Rochester Cathedral. This piece of land, although granted by Offa to the Archbishop of Canterbury, is not only situated within the diocese of Rochester, but is immediately surrounded by the demesnes of Rochester Church. From a realization of the above three land-marks of the charter, it is certain that, although Cliffe is not named, the site of the church and town of Cliffe itself, as well as Higham, is included within

[1] Sheet 1.   [2] Hist. of Kent, vol. I., p. 526-7.
[3] See also " Willelmus de Cloeville duas partes decime de Acle." (Mon. Angl., vol. I.. 169.)   [4] Cod. Dip. CXXI.

the land-marks of the grant; and that the granted manor is
identical with those parishes, as they have afterwards become.
Cooling adjoins the granted land to the east ; Acleag, now Oakley,
to the south ; Merston, is described by Hasted as a forgotten
parish, and no longer appears even in his own map of the
Hundred, but he identifies the ruined church among the buildings
of " Green Farm," close to Gads-hill.   From this he represents it
to have reached the Shorne Marshes ; that is to the Thames
shore ; forming, therefore, the western boundary of Cliffe and
Higham, and including the already mentioned detachment of
Chalk parish, and having Acleag named as one of its boundaries.[1]

In this charter of Offa, we see one of the examples of those first
separations of land, which afterwards became what we call a
parish.   What we now call a parish, is not an invention or
institution by Archbishop Honorius, or Archbishop Theodore, nor
of any individual genius ; any more than shires and hundreds
were invented by King Alfred.   Our parishes are the natural and
exigent result of the variety of causes that have planted churches;
to the use of which, and to the privileges of the cures vested in
them, neighbours have acquired customary or other rights.
Territorial parishes are definitions and ratifications of these
emergent rights, that pre-existed, as other political results do pre-
exist, such confirmations of them.   Their multiplication may
have been promoted, more or less, by different men in different
ages, including our own age.   We shall presently see, that
it is most likely that Offa founded the church at Cliffe ; and
this charter no doubt fixes the date of it.   Higham must have
been separated from it, into another parish, at a later time.
The Archbishop of Canterbury continued to be the owner of
Cliffe until K. Henry VIII.; and the rectory is still in the gift
of the Archbishop, and exempt from Rochester which encompasses

[1] Hasted (vol. I. p. 531.) quotes a charter of Æthelred, A.D. 1001,
granting to the Priory of Canterbury "Terram Clofiæ." That is, apparently, regranting to his newly instituted monks, this very piece of land
which Offa had earlier granted to the secular church. If so, the orthography "Clofia," points to its identity with "Cloveshoe." The nature of
the document quoted by Hasted, may be gathered from a contemporary
one of the same kind, printed in the Monasticon. Vol. I. p. 99. No. V.

it   As Johnson of Cranbrook himself admits, "It is indeed a parish most singularly exempt; for the incumbent is the Archbishop's immediate surrogate."

But there is a much later Mercian council, which deserves to be noticed; not for its intrinsic importance, but on account of the place from which it is dated.[1] It is a sale of two bits of land at Canterbury to the Archbishop, A.D. 823, by Ceoluulf, "rex merciorum seu etiam cantwariorum." The price seems to have been, a pot of gold and silver money, by estimation five pounds and-a-half (or? four and-a-half); more portable and convenient to Ceoluulf under Bcornuulf's usurpation of Mercia. This was just when Mercia was waning, and Wessex ascendant. The date is "in uillo regali. qui dicitur werburging wic." It will be remembered what was the business that first called us to the Kentish Hoo: the finding one of our St. Werburgh dedications there.

That this Werburghwick was in the Hoo, will become more likely by comparison with another charter.[2] This is, a grant of a privilege to the Bishop of Rochester, by Æthelbald, A.D. 734, which has an endorsed confirmation, by Beorhtuulf "regi mcrcioru in uico regali uuerbergeuuic," which endorsement must have been added about A.D. 844. Turn also to the Anglo-Saxon Chronicle, A.D. 851 or 853, where it is said that the Heathen men having held their winter in Thanet; in the same year came 350 ships into Thames mouth, and broke Canterbury, and London, and made this same Beorhtuulf King of the Mercians fly with his army, and went south over Thames into Surrey.[3] It is thought more likely that he was at his villa regalis, in the Hoo, than at Tamworth; where however he sometimes is also found.

The truth seems to be, that, when Mercia relapsed into a mere province or Ealdormanship, it still retained its hold in Kent as an appanage. Thus we have seen Ceoluulf at our Werburghwick in the Hoo, A.D. 823; and Beorhtwulf in the same place, A.D. 844, and again, apparently disturbed by the Danes, A.D. 853. In the

---

[1] Cod. Dip., No. ccxvii.   [2] C. D., No. lxxviii.

[3] There is some difference of this statement among the six texts. Some include London, and some do not.

paper, before referred to, Mr. Rashleigh has given an analytical
table of a hoard of about 550 Anglo-Saxon Coins found at or near
Gravesend in 1838, which must have been buried so late as A.D.
874-5. Of these 429 are of Burgred king of Mercia A.D. 852-874,
and one of Ceoluulf (II.) of Mercia, A.D. 874. Probably the
boundary of the latest holding of Mercians in Kent, answers to
that of the diocese of Rochester, as it came down to the middle
of the present century ; somewhat abnormally consisting of only
a part of a county. Dioceses were originally identical with civil
provinces ; and have been dormantly conservative of their bound-
aiies, during those very times when political revolutions have been
most active upon those of civil states.

It thus appears, that the three most frequent of the names,
from which the series of Mercian synods are dated, can be
accounted for as of places practically in the same locality ; and
that, the one to which tradition, before it had been tampered with
by philological evolution, had already directly pointed ; and on a
piece of land, exceptionally given to Canterbury, encompassed by
the lands of Rochester, for a purpose of which the circumstances
here adduced are the only explanation and index. It is not
inferred that all three names indicate the same building : probably
not ; for, in a later synod, "ad Clobeham," (A.D. 825)[1] a judgment
"prius at Cælchythe" is referred to. But so might, up to our
time, a judgment at Westminster, or at Guildhall, be quoted in
the Chancellor's Court at Lincoln's Inn ; but all three would be at
London.

Although the synods of the series are most frequently dated
from Cloveshoe, Chalkhythe, and Acleah, other places have one or
two each. There is "Berhford," A.D 685, usually placed at
Burford, Oxon., for no other reason than the sound of the name,
connected with the old prejudice for that neighbourhood as central
for Mercia. "Baccanceld," A.D. 798, was certainly in Kent, since
there was also a council of the still self-acting king of Kent held
there, A.D. 694. Another name "Bregentforda," very doubtfully,

---

[1] Cod. Dip., No. MXXXIV.

upon no better ground, placed at Brentford. All these deserve to
be closely re-considered ; and if possible supported by some reason,
added to these guesses from the merest outside likeness in the
names.

Already, A.D. 680, Theodore, Archbishop of Canterbury, had
presided at a general Council of the Bishops of England, said by
Ven. Beda to be "in loco qui Saxonico vocabulo *Haethfelth* nom-
inatur." Some have placed this at one of the various Hatfields
or Heathfields that may have struck the taste of either ; whether
in Yorkshire, Herts, Essex, Sussex, or Somerset. But Archbishop
Parker[1] says that it was "juxta Roffam," apparently quoting
"Roff. Histor." This, at any rate, shews that near Rochester was
at least not thought an unlikely place for a great general Council.
Collier also gives the marginal title "The synod at Hatfield *or*
Clyff, near Rochester." So much for Heathfelth. But where, after
all, was "Herutford," the place of the earlier synod (A.D. 673),
also convened by Archbishop Theodore ? This may be looked upon
as the initial one of the long series of "Clofeshoch" synods : at
which that series was first appointed. Mr. Kemble says[2] that it
was "presided over by Hlothari the sovereign of Kent," and this
was probably the case, although Beda does not expressly say so.
Beda only adds, to his account of the decrees of the council, a
paragraph beginning with a statement that it was held A.D. 673,
the year in which king Ecgberct had died and been succeeded by
his brother Hlothere. Kent was still an independent kingdom ;
and, not only in the primacy, but in its instrument, the series of
synods thus instituted, possessed within itself the heart of the
now established church ; which, having become an active political
function of concentration, was a much coveted constituent of
empire ; and invited the impending aggression of Mercia. Within
three years of the first institution and localisation of these councils, Æthelred made a direct swoop upon this quarry, when he
entered Kent at this very Hoo, the appointed place of the future
councils.

The only reason for "Hertford," as the usual interpretation
of "Herutford," is again the mere likeness of the name ; and is

[1] De Ant. Brit. Eccl., ed. Drake., p. 81.　　[2] C.D., vol. I., Int. p cvii.

D

not a strong one even of its kind. Any place with " Rod-,"
" Reed-," " Rote-," and many the like initial syllable, would have
a better claim. It is very much suspected that the method,
hitherto practised of placing these old place-names, has been far
too hasty. It may fairly be expected that some of them are no
longer represented by any existing names. We have seen above
by how close a shaving several have survived. But of this name
" Herutford," " Heorotford," or " Heortford," it might safely be
assumed that the initial " He-," is no more than a prefixed
aspirate : that it is not of the essence of the name. And so Beda
himself evidently thought ; for when[1] he mentions a name, almost
identical with this one, in Hampshire ; he gives it with a Latin
explanation, " *Hreutford*, id est *Vadum harundinis*," evidently
taking it for Reed or Rodford.[2] We might also expect to find
such a name represented by a modern name beginning with " Wr- ; "
but an inconsiderable " Redham," a farm, in Gloucestershire, is
found written " Hreodham " in the tenth century.

The above had already been written, when it seemed to be at
least a formal obligation to test this principle, by a direct appli-
cation of it to the district under consideration ; which has
unexpectedly yielded, what is at any rate, an example of the
principle. Whether or not it indicates an actual trace of the place
" Herutford " itself, shall not at present be ventured to say.
However,[3] in the charter, dated 778, already quoted, in which the

---

[1] Lib. IV., ch. 15.

[2] Looking at this again, a fresh and interesting association arises.
This must have been at or close to "*Red*bridge," at the head of the
Southampton estuary. Beda is telling the story of the two young pagan
Jutish princes, from the Isle of Wight, being baptised, preparatory to their
martyrdom, by Cyniberet abbot of Hreutford. Close to Redbridge is
Nutshalling, the monastery to which the young Winfred, afterwards St.
Bonifatius, passed from Exeter to the care of the abbot " Wynbert."
There can be no doubt that Beda's monastery of Hrentford is identical
with the Nutschalling of the biographers of Winfred ; and that Beda's
" Cyniberet " is the same as their " Wynbert."

If this identification, both of a place and a person, that have both been
known by different names for above a thousand years, should be justified ;
it will be all the more remarkable, because Beda's text has been in English
keeping ; whilst that of the biographers of Bonifatius has been chiefly in
foreign literary custody.   [3] Cod. Dip., No. CXXXII.

level land north of Cliffe is called "Scaga;" the land-marks begin
with the words "Huic uero terrae adiacent pratae ubi dicitur
Hreodham." The land itself, to which it is adjacent, is called
"Bromgeheg;" a name which now remains as "Broomey," a
house only, at Cooling; and the chief land-limits are "Clifwara
gemære" and "Culinga gemære." The land is granted to the
Bishop of Rochester, but evidently adjoins the eastern side of
that including Cliffe itself, which had already been given to the
Archbishop, as above quoted.

Even at first sight it would seem unaccountable, that, at a
synod held at Hertford; what appears to amount to a periodical
series of repetitions or continuations, or in fact adjournments of it
should have been determined upon at so distant a place as
Clofeshoch,—wherever that may prove to have been—must have
been from Hertford. It would seem more likely, that the future
place of assembly in view, would have been practically in the same
place. This initial council was under the presidency of the
Primate; and so were those that followed, except that when the
King of Mercia was present the Primate yielded the first place to
him The permanently appointed place would also be likely to
have in view the convenience of access, to the Primate, of his
suffragans, from all the sub-kingdoms; and to this the Watling-
street contributed, not only his own ready approach from Canterbury, to the very place where tradition has fixed it; but also, for
those who were to meet him there; the most perfect road from
London, and the entire north-west of the island; whilst immediate
access from East Saxony, East Anglia, and the northern dioceses,
has been shewn in the well frequented ferry, also to this very
place. The Church of England is seen to have had an earlier
approximation towards political unity than the Kingdom of
England. The former was, in fact, contributory to the latter as,
perhaps, one of its most efficient causes. This was not lost sight
of by those who aimed at the supremacy; whose policy, therefore,
was to have the Primate at his right hand in his councils; and to
cultivate an identity of interest with him. Offa's attempt to set up

an Archbishop at Lichfield, only seven miles from his home-court at Tamworth, was in this direction.

This attempt to determine the true place of these synods, during the continuance of Mercian supremacy in England ; was intended to confirm the statement, that wherever extraneous dedications of St. Werburgh are found, traces are also found of the energetic or active presence of Æthelbald. It may seem to be rather an elaborate implement for so small a purpose. It has been more extensive than was contemplated : but, if once success-fully constructed, it may serve a greater purpose of its own : the setting at rest of a long dispute. And this purpose of its own will itself receive back all that it gives to ours : for if the presence of Æthelbald, accounts for our having found a St. Werburgh in this now secluded peninsula; the presence of that dedication, is a weighty confirmation of the much disputed fact, that he was busy and much resident there ; and that we might reasonably expect his most important acts to be dated thence. At all events, it is hoped that our sixth and last remaining of the wandering dedi-cations of St. Werburgh, in the Kentish Hoo, has been thus discovered to have been in the immediate company of Æthelbald ; when, as it is said in the Anglo-Saxon Chronicle :

> " A.D. 742. Now was a great synod gathered at Cloneshou, and there was Æthelbald, King of the Mercians, and Cutbert, Archbishop, and many other wise men."

But something more is to be said concerning this passage itself of the Chronicle. It appears to be only contained in one manu-script ; consequently in the five-column edition, this year is only filled in in the fifth column ; the other four being blank. Sir T. D. Hardy says of this solitary manuscript, that it is " apparently of the twelfth century ;" and that it contains " various peculiar additions, chiefly relating to Kentish ecclesiastical affairs."[1] Pro-fessor Earle also says of it : " There is no external tradition informing us as to what home it belonged, but the internal

---

[1] M. H. B., Pref. 77.

evidence assigns it to Christ Church, Canterbury."[1] This is much more to our purpose than if it had been in all the manuscripts : for if it had been a part of the usual and received text of the Chronicle, it would have here been a mere retranscription, for ages, with an indefinite locality. As it is, standing only in a Chronicle of Canterbury ; it had evidently claimed the special attention of the Annalist, from its direct local Kentish interest ; and especially its concern with a piece of land, which, we have seen, was owned by the Cathedral Church to which the writer belonged. What has been already said about the " Dr. Hethe " note[2] applies with still greater force to this; which is indeed the same Canterbury tradition ; only that it is in hand-writing of four hundred years earlier date.

But " Hoo-St.-Werburgh " is a parish adjoining to Cliffe ; and our argument is, that when, as recorded in the Canterbury copy of the Chronicle, A.D. 742, there was a synod at Cloueshou, and that " Æthelbald was there ; " he founded and dedicated this church, as we have found him to have done elsewhere. Added to this, we have seen reason, and shall presently see more, that the neighbouring church of Cliffe itself was founded by his great successor Offa, A.D. 774. It has been said, and with great likelihood, that Cliffe and Hoo-St.-Werburgh were the two most ancient churches in the Hoo ; and that they are the mother churches of the five or six others in the peninsula, that have sprung up at some later times ; their segregated portions, which, in due course, have consolidated into separate parishes.

As before said, the church at Cliffe-at-Hoo itself, has the dedication of St. Helen ; and it is believed that, by a similar foretaste of chivalry, to that of Æthelbald's for St. Werburgh ; Offa habitually planted his standard under the name of this other female saint. It is, therefore, no wonder that we find these two, close together, in that very district wherein, during two long reigns, Æthelbald and Offa are recorded as constantly performing acts of sovereignty. Of this there are many evidences, besides the councils about which we are engaged, in the accounts of their

---

[1] Two Chron., Introd., lii.   [2] P, 23.

dealings, in this district, and along the Medway, and throughout Kent, in the manner in which conquerors usually deal with newly-acquired land ; as shewn in their numerous charters.

The reputed British-Roman nativity of St. Helen in Deira, appears to have given her name a prevalence in that province, with which the Anglian successors of the northern Britons were infected ; like that of St. Alban, and the Kentish St. Martin, with his prolific eastern grafts.[1] And they accepted and improved the legacy. But the remains, of this acceptance, of a local aspect · of religion, are the most conspicuous in Deira ; and in Lindisse or Southumbria, a constituent of that kingdom. It did not extend to Bernicia. Of the known existing dedications of St. Helen, Durham contains only two, Northumberland one, Westmoreland and Cumberland none ; and we learn from Bp. Forbes, that the name thinly re-appears beyond the border in Scottish Northumbria. But in Yorkshire we find twenty-two, and in Lincolnshire thirty ; and these last, except two a little south of it, are all in Lindsey proper : Nottinghamshire also has ten. Lancashire has four or five. The tendency of Northumbrian hagiology to spread into Mercia proper, has been already mentioned ; and a still pretty free, but reduced, scattering of St. Helens is found in that kingdom. Derbyshire has 5, Cheshire 3, Northants 6, Leicestershire 4, but Staffordshire none, Salop one—being near to [H]Elle[n]smere. Bedfordshire one at [H]El[len]stow. Herts one at Wheathampstead—near Offa's St. Alban, and Essex (Colchester) one. The Wiccian counties, Warwick two, Worcester (city), and Gloucestershire (north) each one.

The above examples, of this dedication in England—about 96—have been recited, chiefly for the purpose of exhaustion. The residual seven or eight, still more scattered over the more southern counties, are what our lesson must be chiefly read from ; that they are found in the footsteps of Offa, as marks of new possession ; in a similar manner to the St. Werburghs in the tract of Æthelbald. No doubt each of the ninety six has its own story to tell, but it does not now concern us.

[1] Kent has 15 extant St. Martins, Lincoln 14, Norfolk 14, Suffolk 7, Essex 4, Middlesex 8.

As we have already seen,[1] A.D. 774, Offa granted the land at Higham in Hoo, which includes the site of the church and town of Cliffe, to Jaenberht, Archbishop of Canterbury; exceptionally surrounded by lands of the Bishop of Rochester. At the same time, there can be no doubt, he founded and dedicated the church, which still bears the name of St. Helen. Again, in the Anglo-Saxon Chronicle, A.D. 777, it is written, " Now Cynewulf " —of Wessex—" and Offa fought around Bensington, and Offa took that town." The church at Bensington on the left—or Offa's —shore of the Thames is also a St. Helen at this day. At Albury, also in Oxfordshire, about nine miles north of Bensington, on the smaller river Thame, the church is St Helen. Also, on the Thames, at Abingdon, as is well known, there is a St. Helen. With regard, however, to this last, the local monastic tradition gives an earlier origin, founded on a miraculous discovery of a Holy Rood. This must stand, against our use of this example, for whatever the tradition may be worth. Perhaps a fourth " Sancta Helena " is recorded,[2] as the sanctuary of a fugitive who had stolen a bridle, A.D. 995. The land, given in conciliation, must have been close to the chalk ridge south of the White Horse Vale, Berks; as, among the boundaries, is " Cwicelmes hlæw," well known to be on this ridge; and the " grenanweg," still called by the neighbours "the Green Way;" being a part of what is called " the Drover's Road," by which, until outdone by the rail, cattle from the west were driven, for many miles, turnpike free, and with peripatetic grazing. The St. Helen here referred to may, however, have been Abingdon itself.

At any rate, here are three, out of the few existing southern St. Helens, in the line of frontier then realised by Offa against Wessex. The same line of St. Helens, both eastward and westward, is also extended across the island, from the extreme north of Kent, as we have seen; by the well-known one in London; and another formerly at Malmsebury, and another at Bath. These last three—making six—also probably resulted from the same campaign of Offa as the Berkshire and Oxfordshire ones.

[1] P. 45.　　　[2] Cod. Dip., No. MCCLXXXIX.

That at Bath, however, has a special claim to our attention ;
having been in that same suburb outside the north gate, where
also was found the St. Werburgh, within the fork of the Foss-
way and that now called Via Julia.   Here then, as already in the
Hoo of Kent, we once more find a St. Werburgh and a St. Helen
in immediate companionship.   The seal of Æthelbald endorsed by
that of Offa, the inheritor of his policy.[1]   But what is the signifi-
cance of these emblems of Mercian territory, being both found
outside the Roman walled town on the north side ?   Did this
suburb become specially a Mercian quarter ?   The monastery, of
which Offa was a reputed founder or re-founder about this very
time, must have been a chief occupant of the area within the
walls ; and its possessions extended, in the opposite direction,
beyond the river, on the Wessex side.   We have already seen[2]
signs of Æthelbald's further south-west progress along the Foss-
way as far as into East Devon.

Besides this line of St. Helens, along the frontier, which was
the result of the campaign recorded in the Chronicle, under A.D.
777 ; there are still three outlying southward, along the south coast :
the extreme natural limit of the Saxon nations.   Although not
recorded in the Anglo-Saxon Chronicle, an earlier excursion of
Offa is mentioned by others.   A.D. 771, Simeon of Durham[3] says
"His diebus Offa, rex Merciorum, Hestingorum gentem armis
subegerat."   Dr. Lappenberg, in relating this feat of Offa's, calls
"the Hestingas, a people whose locality, like that of so many
others among the Saxons, is not known with certainty.   They
have been sought for about Hastings in Sussex, and most probably
inhabited the district around that town to which they gave their
name."[4]   Roger of Wendover, however, reads "Anglorum gentem."[5]   Upon this, Sir F. Palgrave had already noted : "It is

---

[1] These were both in that suburb, still called "Ladymead."   But it
would be one of the rash things, that are so often committed in these
matters, to connect this name with the two Lady dedications.   In fact
there is a tolerable alternative.   It may have been a mead that belonged to
one "Godric Ladda," a witness to an Anglo-Saxon manumission of a
Bondsman, in Bath Abbey. (Hickes, Dissert., 8 Epist., p. 22).

[2] P. 124-5.   [3] Mon. Hist. Brit., p. 664,

[4] A.-S. K., I., 229-30.   [5] Flores Hist., 1601. p. 143.

not easy to ascertain what people are meant. The name has inclined many writers to suppose that they were the inhabitants of Hastings, but they could scarcely be of sufficient importance. Perhaps we should read *East Anglorum.*[1] Other recent historians, with or without hesitation, adopt the present town of Hastings as the scene of the conquest.

Here then we have another fully ripe historic doubt; so evenly balanced in the judgments of the most specifically learned, that after what has already been shewn, of the local coincidences of dedications of St Helen with the feats of Offa; if the like should be found also to apply to the one here recorded, would be sufficient to give a considerable bias to the scale. And this is what we do find.

About a mile north of the town, which still bears a name that has since acquired other claims to places in history, Hastings; is a village called Ore; of which the church has another of our southern outlying dedications of St. Helen. If Offa's conquest, as recorded by Simeon of Durham, refers to Sussex, it needs only to say so much, in order to account for this one; and to fulfil the promise of our theory; that the name of this saint and the written witnesses of Offa's progress, shall be found to mutually confirm each other as evidence of his active presence. This village is situated on an elevation commanding the town itself; and on the southern edge of a ridge, along which, and close to the village, runs one of those great roads, of which the straight line is significant of a long, ancient, and arterial use. In fact it must have been always the almost sole approach to the town, whether from Kent or from the centre of England. Moreover, at whatever point of the neighbouring beach, at a later time, William landed; this road must have been his principal means of reaching Battle. Here, therefore, upon the door itself of the town, still remains the usual seal of Offa's conquests. Sir Francis Palgrave's objection, of the insufficient importance of the Gens Hestingorum, would not, it is thought, have been raised, if he had remembered that the large territory, called the "Rap de Hastings" of Domesday, and the

[1] Eng. Com., Proofs, cclxxix.

Rape of Hastings of our own time, most likely had already existed
from the first settlement of the South Saxons. Two or three
years later, Offa is still found busy in that part of Kent which
adjoins this most eastern of the Rapes of Sussex.

But although the Hæstingas only are mentioned, as the people
first encountered, there are other evidences that he extended his
conquests westward throughout Sussex. One of his St. Helens
remains on the foot of the South Downs, between the peninsulated
stronghold called The Devil's Dike and the sea ; and, within
actual eyeshot, is another, on the opposite eastern coast of the
Isle of Wight. Moreover.he has, as was his practice in many parts
of England, also left his own name along the line, in Offham, near
Lewes, Offington, near Worthing, Offham, close to Arundel Park.

There are also one or two St. Helens or Elens, both in Cornwall and Wales : which would be in accordance with what otherwise
has been said above, but as several local Celtic saints have names
liable to become more familiar by corruption into this one, they
will not be here called into evidence.

For the series of synods of which the acts are dated from
Cloveshoe did not cease with the reign of Æthelbald. These,
interspersed with occasional dates of Cealchythe and Aclea, continued throughout the other long and dominant Mercian reign of
his successor Offa. Indeed they continued as long as Mercia
remained supreme, and far into the ninth century : the date of
" Clofeshoe " being last met with for a synod under Beornnulf,
A.D. 825 : about the time when both Kent and Essex are found to
have been annexed by Wessex.

It may seem difficult to realise that what is a small detached
region—almost practically an island—now containing only four or
five villages or decayed towns ; was, for about a century and a
half, the seat of one of the royal residences, where a succession
of powerful kings held so many of their courts to which were
convened the magnates of their own and of subject kingdoms.
The truth is, that political centrality is not coincident with
geographical ; and is only partially dependent upon natural aspect
or condition. London is very far from a geographical centre ; and,

if we could bring into view its original natural aspect ; London, with its marshes would be as incredible as the place here concerned. Its present greatness is the outgrowth of the later supremacy of Wessex ; and London was as much an outpost of Saxony into Mercia, as the Hoo had been of Anglia into Centland.

Those who expect a confirmation of this regal occupation of the Hoo, from substantial remains there, may remember that a thousand years of desertion have passed over it. As Fuller said, when writing of this controversy about Cloveshoe, already warm in his day :[1] " Nor doth the modern Meanness of the Place make anything against it ; it might be a Gallant in that Age, which is a Beggar now-a-dayes." Geographical and natural conditions have much to do with the choice and permanence of the seats of governments ; but political needs and fortunes often over-rule or reverse them. The rise of Wessex turned the preference to other centres ; and the exposure of this peninsula to the ravages of the Danes, just then becoming active, is sufficient to have brought desolation upon it. The site of New York seems very much like this ; but its growth was not prevented by such a constant peril as this last in its front, nor by the ascendancy of a rival power in its rear. It is political causes that have surrounded the circular mound at Windsor with the regal associations, which have forsaken that of Tamworth ; and the same political causes have covered with houses and palaces, not only the elevated spot upon which London was first planted, but the many miles of swamp that encompassed it. When cities, or settlements upon elevations, take to growing great, they no longer despise the alluvial levels which skirt them ; but cover even these with buildings. This is the case with London itself, where even the supreme Aula Regia of the Saxon empire, that has inherited the " England " of Æthelbald and Offa ; stands upon a similar alluvial appendage of the higher ground of the original settlement; to that which, projecting from the chalky heights of the Hoo, has been declared to be inconsistent with its history.

Again, are there preserved, anywhere at all, any fragments whatever, of masonry of the time of Æthelbald and Offa, even

[1] Ch. II., 1655, II., VIII., 21.

under the most favourable circumstances ? We have seen that many churches were founded in that age, that have continued in vital existence to this day. In these, if anywhere, remains of the first structures might have been found. Instead of this, the few præ-Norman relics that do exist can scarcely be said to approach that date ; and when, later, they do crop up ; they seem to bring with them an indication, why they are the earliest. They are found in places where stone is as plenty and as easily hewn as wood ; and they appear to be worked and constructed by hands and heads that had been accustomed to work and construct in wood ; and often with adze-like tool marks. The angry question whether the word " timber " was, by birth, a verb or a noun—a question of which some of the most eminent Anglo-Saxon scholars seem, on waking, to have found themselves on the wrong side—shall not here be roused ; but the absence of earlier remains may be accounted for, by taking for granted, wood to have been, at the earlier time, the material mostly used. What then can we expect to find in a tract of land, ever since abandoned to its ordinary rural and pastoral condition ? The cartular evidence of the importance of this small territory, during the time in question, is most abundant ; and the many traces of antiquity, in the names of now inconsiderable spots, has been already referred to.

As the inferences, from the surviving examples of these dedications, and their topographical distribution, may have assumed the tone of exact or statistical inductions ; it is but right that they should be qualified by an admission that, from that point of view, they are subject to some elements of discount. It has been already admitted that more extinct St. Werburghs may come to light ; and of course it is impossible to foresee to what extent the inferences may be thereby disturbed ; although it is not expected that they can be substantially over-balanced. Indeed, there are not wanting other spots which have names with a suspicious possibility of being corruptions of the name of Werburgh, similar to those that we have seen, where they are confirmed by the actual survival of the dedication itself ; as in the cases of Warburton and Warbstow. Of these are two eminences, the situations of which are strikingly similar to that at Wembury, as if chosen by the same eye. They are close to the sea shore, but in other parts of the south coast. These are a hill, called " Warberrys," close to Torquay; and another called " Warbarrow," in the isle of Purbeck. But neither of these have traces of the dedication, and both names are quite likely to have had other causes; nor can the places be directly connected with any known record of Æthelbald. Therefore they shall not be enlisted into the present enquiry. There is also a Wareberrewe near Wallingford, with the present dedication of S. Laurence.

The indications, that have been above induced, however, from the occurrences of the dedications of St. Werburgh in south England, as well as those of St. Cuthbert in Wessex, are very distinct and definite as guide-posts in historical topography; being strictly national or dynastic. But St. Helen, as compared with them, has the great disadvantage of being catholic and illustrious ; and the possibility, of course, exists, for a catholic dedication to have had sometimes other causes besides that here attributed—the personal veneration of a conqueror. It is, however, thought that the comparative numbers in the different provinces, that have been offered, may help any judgment upon this point. One cause of aberration, in the case of the St. Helens may be, that some examples may have been "St. Helen and Holy Rood ;" and, as often happens to a joint dedication, one half may have been worn off by grinding time : sometimes the first, sometimes the last ; so that some of what are now only known as Holy Rood, or Holy Cross, may have been originally St. Helens. On the other hand, the dedication of Holy Rood may, in some cases, have been independently attached to churches, that have arisen where there had already been a cross of a martyr, which had brought a great resort to a spot of reputed eminent sanctity.[1] Or, as in the legend

---

[1] The contemporary authoress of the life of St. Willibald, says that (about A.D. 703), it was the custom among the Saxons—*i.e.* Willibald's compatriots in Wessex—for some noble or substantial men, not to erect a church upon their estates, but to hold in honour a lofty Holy Cross. This seems a strong confirmation of a recent suggestion of Prof. Earle, that the English word "Church " is a transliteration, and scarcely that, of the word "crux." It seems to be a more likely word for the churches of Augustine

of Abingdon, where a cross, or a piece of the True Cross has been
said to have been miraculously found : or a wonder-working
Crucifix, as at Waltham Abbey. The local distribution of Holy
Roods does not shew any estimable counter-balance of that of
the St. Helens ; and the Holy Roods themselves are believed to
have had a tendency to pass into St. Saviour, or Christchurch.

One very general agent in the obliteration of those dedications
that are national, or otherwise capable of rendering historical
indications, has been particularly active in the English part of
this island. This is the tendency to depose them, in favour of
the greater saints, who are recognized and honoured throughout
Christendom. This, as might have been expected, is more particularly the case of St. Mary. It is likely that many of the
churches with this dedication are amplifications of sanctuaries of
the more ancient and national kind. So strong was this tendency
that, where it did not drown out the original tutelar name of a
church ; it must at least be satisfied by the addition of a " Lady
Chapel." Such a process of change may often be seen actually
at work. The fine large church at Marden, Herefordshire, is said,
both by Leland and Browne Willis, to have the dedication of St·
Ethelbert ; and so no doubt it has : but the present officers of
the church, if asked, pronounce it to be of St. Mary. A glance at
the building accounts for this. Within the church, at, perhaps,
about twenty feet from the western wall, is preserved an uncommon
relique, the well of St. Ethelbert ; murdered by Offa, about a mile
off, but whose shrine was at Marden, until translated to Hereford
Cathedral. There can be no doubt that the well occupied the
focus of the original small sanctuary that was first raised over the
reliques of the martyr ; and which was on the brink of the river,
that flows near the western front of the church, and so prevented
enlargement in that direction. The large increase of the church
eastward, in accordance with the practice of the later age, having
been devoted to the name of St. Mary. Another similar case, of

and Birinus, than the usual one more distantly derived. Leland in one
place has " curx " for " crux." In planting these crosses, these old
Lords of Manors were sowing the seeds of what are to us parishes.

Middleham in Richmondshire, has been kindly brought to notice by Mr. W. H. D. Longstaffe. The original dedication is St. Alkelda, whose martyrdom ,being strangled by two female servants, is represented on glass. Her traditional altar-tomb, is westward of the chancel arch of the collegiate choir of St. Mary, founded by King Richard III. The only other traces of St. Alkelda is a church in her name at Giggleswick, some miles westward.

That sort of conviction, which arises from a gradual accumu. lation of facts, upon what had at first started as a suspicion or a guess ; cannot be so vividly imparted to a reader. But even if what has been said above should have been successful ; it will be very far from having exhausted the materials of this kind of enquiry : will only have served, by one or two examples, to shew the value of a neglected class of monuments, which, it is thought, have not yet been made to yield up their teaching. At the best, what has here been done, can be no more than the exposure of two or three fragments of a vast ruin, co-extensive with the land ; of which the plan should be restored by a comparative registration or cartography of the whole. In the Celtic portions of these islands, the dedications of the churches retain much of their original or primitive topical distribution ; shewing, as they have sometimes already been made to do, the maternity of missionary centres to offshoot churches. In the Teutonized portions of England, it is likely that they have another and greater lesson. They are here, in addition, believed to be able to shew, to a certain extent, what may be called an ethnical stratification ; which, if carefully observed, would often mark out the extension of revolutions or conquests : more especially in those early times, of which written history is scanty or altogether wanting.

www.ingramcontent.com/pod-product-compliance
Lightning Source LLC
Chambersburg PA
CBHW021534270326
41930CB00008B/1242